WESTLIFE | In Our Own Words

WESTLIFE | In Our Own Words

EUGENE MASTERSON
Foreword by RONAN KEATING

MAINSTREAM
PUBLISHING

EDINBURGH AND LONDON

Acknowledgements

It would have been impossible to produce this book without the dedication of my editors at Mainstream, Sarah Edwards and Joe McAvoy, and the designer of this book, Siân Braes. Also at Mainstream, I'd like to thank directors Bill Campbell and Peter MacKenzie, and publicity manager Sharon Atherton.

A big thanks to Louis Walsh – we go back a long way! I first met Ronan Keating at the Boyzone auditions in Dublin, November 1993, and have known him through good times and bad times. Thanks Ronan.

I'd like to thank all at *Ireland on Sunday*, particularly editor Liam Hayes, news editor Ken Whelan, managing editor Cathal Dervan, and Niamh Hodgins, Donal Dervan and Orla Cooney. Thanks also to Kathryn Mason, Stephen Power and Freddie Middleton at BMG Ireland. Thanks to photographer Andy Earl of BMG for use of the image on page 76.

Anto Byrne, Westlife's tour manager, who had to put up with endless phone calls – thanks Anto. A big thanks to Sharon Tobutt of RCA UK.

I'd also like to thank my family in Swords: Jim, Rosaleen, Sharon and Aoife, and my brother Barry and sister-in-law Jacinta, as well as all my friends.

This book could not have been brought to you without the help of five of the most wonderful women I have had the pleasure of meeting: Patricia Egan, Mae Filan, Mairead McFadden, Yvonne Byrne and Marie Feehily.

Lastly, where would we be without the lads themselves. I found Kian, Nicky, Shane, Bryan and Mark to be five really genuine, friendly and helpful guys. They deserve all the success that comes their way. Thanks lads. Go n-eirigh an bothar libh!

Copyright © Eugene Masterson, 2000
All rights reserved
The moral right of the author has been asserted

First published in Great Britain in 2000 by
MAINSTREAM PUBLISHING COMPANY (EDINBURGH) LTD
7 Albany Street
Edinburgh EH1 3UG

ISBN 1 84018 267 9

No part of this book may be reproduced or transmitted in any form or by any means without written permission from the publisher, except by a reviewer who wishes to quote brief passages in connection with a review written for insertion in a magazine, newspaper or broadcast

A catalogue record for this book is available from the British Library

Typeset in Centaur
Reprographics by Inside Image Ltd, Edinburgh
Printed and bound in Great Britain by Butler & Tanner Ltd, Frome and London

Contents

Foreword

Getting involved with Westlife for me was like being in Boyzone in the beginning all over again. I just noticed this feeling, that there was this hunger within the lads, and it reminded me of how eager and naïve I was way back then. But Westlife have outdone even Boyzone, by having their first three singles go to number one in Britain and Ireland – the first boy band to pull off that feat.

Initially, I didn't want to get involved with managing a band. I've been offered a few bands to manage over the years and lots of bits and bobs, but I've turned them all down. I know most of the lads are big fans of the Backstreet Boys, and one aspect of Westlife that I like is the way they're able to harmonise together. I love all sorts of music.

The plan for Westlife that we set out with was that we wanted to succeed. It was all or nothing; we needed that so badly. When we started out with them there had to be a change in the line-up because Louis and myself weren't altogether happy with the initial band, but I believe we've now got the perfect blend. People may criticise bands like Westlife and Boyzone for being 'manufactured', but the process of getting those people together is really the nurturing and developing of talent and some of the best music today has been created thanks to that process.

I would like to have

a say in the day-to-day management of the band but really, with my workload, it's impossible. I can't give the band the attention that Louis (Walsh, Boyzone manager) can. But I try and keep in touch most days with Anto (Byrne, Westlife's tour manager) and the lads.

I myself have my début solo album coming out in February 2000 and I have been busy writing and recording it in Nashville, America, with my good friends Barry and Andy Gibb of The Bee Gees. Hopefully, Boyzone will have another new album out towards the end of 2000.

Myself, my wife Yvonne and our son Jack are keeping well. Music will always be my life; I don't want this to be a short-term thing. As for Westlife: I honestly think they're going to be one of the most successful pop bands ever.

Ronan Keating

Kian Egan

Family

I grew up in Sligo, which is a provincial town in the west of Ireland. My fellow band members Mark Feehily and Shane Filan are also from Sligo, while the other two lads in Westlife, Nicky Byrne and Bryan McFadden, are both from Dublin.

I've got three brothers and three sisters. Colm, the youngest, is five and he's just started school. Then I've got a 13-year-old sister, Marielle, who is into music herself. She was in a girl band, but they were just having a bit of a laugh with each other. She plays the piano and the violin and can sing. She's got a good head on her shoulders.

I think my being in Westlife can be difficult for her. At the start she must have been going, 'Oh, my God, my brother is doing this, that and the other,' you know. It's very hard for her, because if you can imagine her friends, all they might want to talk to her about is the band and stuff like that. I can imagine that getting to her now and again.

Then I've got a 22-year-old brother, Tom. He's big into music as well. He plays in a rock band called Fiction – a very, very good rock band. They're just going into the studio at the moment. He's 100 per cent behind me. He likes our music, I like his music. I shared a bedroom with Tom for most of my life, so we're very close.

When we were growing up he used to be a heavy metaller and he got me into heavy metal too when I was a kid – I used to have long hair and all that! – so when we got separate rooms I started getting into acting.

I was already into acting and playing piano and guitar and all that, because I used to play the piano with my first rock band, Pyromania. Actually, my rock band and Tom's rock band were once in competition against each other. The two bands were in a talent contest and they came first and we came second – but they only just beat us. Fiction are doing really, really well now and it looks like they're going to get a big record deal in America.

Then there's Fenella. She's 23 now. She was a legal secretary but she's got problems with her back so she's not allowed to sit in a chair for more than four hours at a time and she had to give that up. My next brother is Gavin, who's 28 now. He's a professional musician. He went to music college and got an honours degree and now he teaches piano at a college in Sheffield. Gavin taught me how to play the piano when I was a kid, from the age of eight until I was about 16. The same with the guitar, so that's how I learnt how to play.

is Patricia. We're just a basic family, an everyday family living on an estate in Sligo. I simply got a very, very lucky break.

I think my mother made it all happen for me because she put me on stage when I was four years of age, reciting poetry. Then she got my older brother to play the piano and he started teaching me the piano because he was a professional teacher by the age of 18. She also made sure I got guitar lessons, saxophone lessons, clarinet lessons. I did a series of different things so I think she pushed me all my life. She got me into drama and acting and she got me into speech and drama classes, all that kind of stuff.

One poem I can remember reciting publicly when I was younger was called 'Tom's Bomb', written by David Hornsby. I used to do a poem all the time at the *Feis* [an Irish music and poetry competition] and that was always my best poem. I said it about three years constantly from the age of four and I used to do very well as there were different judges each year!

It does help me with lyric writing. When it comes to writing music, I use the piano, I don't just sit down and think of something in my head. I play the piano for a few minutes and then I get a tune in my head and I start writing lyrics to the melody of the song.

Bryan and I wrote a really good song called 'Fragile Heart'; we're going to try and get it on one of our singles. I've written about twenty songs. But the thing about songwriting is it gets better and better as you keep going. You

Bryan can also play a little guitar. I'm teaching Nicky piano at the moment and I'm teaching Shane a bit of guitar. I wouldn't say I'm an accomplished player. I've done grades – grade eight in piano and grade three in guitar – but I'm a rock guitarist, I'm not a classical guitarist. I'm one of those guys with an electric guitar who plugs it in and plays guitar solos all day. That's what I love, playing the guitar.

But Bryan's quite nifty with the guitar too, he's good at chords and stuff like that, and Mark's good at the piano as well, so I wouldn't say I'm the only person that can play but I am the only person who has played since child-hood.

Then there's Vivienne, she's just gone 30. She's a town planner and is now based in Roscommon. There's a bit of an age gap between myself and Vivienne and Gavin, so I'm not as close to them as the younger ones.

I've also got two nephews and one niece: Gavin's married and he's got one little boy. Fenella's unmarried but she's got a little boy and a little girl.

I grew up beside the Showgrounds, a place called Linndale. I grew up very closely with two of my cousins, Michael and Gillian Walsh. They lived just around the corner from me. I was very, very close to Gillian. We did everything together; we used to go down town together and we were both big into all the musicals. I had a great childhood. Gillian was into dancing and all the musicals and stage work and that's what we used to do. We would do a lot of variety shows together and we used to mess about in local community halls, teaching kids how to dance.

My dad works in the ESB [Electricity Supply Board]. His name is Kevin and he's an electrician. My mum's a housewife – her name

don't start writing great songs straight-away, you've got to practise at it and it takes a while and you've got to have structures in your head as well, thinking where to put what, as in, 'OK, we start off like this'. All the boys write songs with me. I do the piano stuff and they do the lyrics or whatever.

School

I started off in a primary school called Scoil Ursula in Sligo and then I went to St John's. I had to move because Scoil Ursula only take boys from junior infants to first class.

I remember my first day in school. My cousin and I were fighting. I had two best friends and I wanted one of them to sit to my left and the other to my right and they wanted the same. But my cousin wanted to sit where I was and I remember fighting with him that day. That's the only thing I recall from my first day! I remember primary school quite well. Miss Barry taught me when I was four or five. Then Miss O'Grady taught me when I was in first class while Miss Dolan taught me when I was in second. Mr Mulhern was quite good; he taught me for fifth and sixth class. He introduced me to Gaelic football and I played a lot of that. He also knew I liked acting as I was going

to drama lessons. We used to do plays every year and I got the lead part in my first play which immediately gave me confidence – if I got the lead part in my first play then I must be good – and so I kept getting lead roles in all the plays.

Secondary school was quite mad. A lot of Gaelic football was involved. I went to Summerhill College in Sligo and the first year there I set up a band called Scrod. There were three of us – myself, Finian Gunning and Derek Lacey. I played guitar and sang. The school put on a rock concert that year and we were actually good enough to play. We used to sing 'Wild Thing' and we changed the lyrics of the song to 'Wild Thing, you make my balls swing'. We also did a song from AC/DC called 'TNT'. That's when I got into the whole 'playing the guitar in a band' thing and I kept doing it until I was about 17. I was a big fan of Bon Jovi, Metallica, Guns 'N Roses. I wasn't into 'heavy, heavy' stuff, but I liked rock music.

In secondary school I never really had any favourite subjects. I liked art because it wasn't just 'study, study, study'. I was never a studier. I liked English, to a certain extent, because I used to like hearing stories and stuff like that. Construction studies, that was good, because there was mechanical drawing involved and again it wasn't 'study, study, study'. I did my Junior Cert [similar to O-levels] and my Leaving Cert [similar to A-levels]. I passed both of them, but I just wasn't a study freak. I didn't like sitting in every night studying for four hours.

I still think everybody should go to school, because you need an education. For me now there's a lot of money in what we do and if I hadn't been to school I wouldn't know how to handle certain types of situation, such as splitting money up if money comes into the gig. There's a lot of business involved, there's accounting involved, there's lawyers involved; there's business involved in every little thing in the world that you make money from so you have to go to school to learn about that.

In school, I met Shane when I was quite young, 12 or 13. He was a year ahead of me though. That's when I started getting into music, although I was already involved. But he got into musicals when he was about 12 or 13 so I got to know him quite well. Mark was in my year, so I already knew him, although I wasn't good mates with him at this stage.

Then, when I was about 16, Shane and I became best friends and we did a musical in school. Then Mark came in and we did another musical and Mark became one of our mates as well.

We did three versions of *Grease* when we were younger.

The first one was in school; that's where Shane and I met Mark and that's how we came to know Mark as a singer. We all played lead roles. Shane was Danny and I was Kenickie. It was after the last night of *Grease* that we started singing at a party. Somebody said, 'You should take it further' and that's when the whole band started. Then *Grease* went back on for the second time in the local theatre, the Hawkswell. We did the whole play and we did a few Backstreet Boys songs, 'I'll Never Break Your Heart' and 'We've Got It Going On', during the interval.

Apart from the local *Grease*, there was the annual school play that we did and we also staged productions such as *The Pyjama Game*, *Oliver*, *Annie* and *West Side Story*. I did about ten of them.

I once dressed up as Marilyn Monroe and I also dressed up as Cilla Black and I have to say I was quite good at both of them. I had two big balloons up my dress, a blonde wig and a beauty spot and I hitched the dress up so you could see my boxer shorts underneath!

Acting has always been important to me: when I was nine years of age I was a dancer in the choruses, when I was 12 I started getting little parts and it just kept growing, growing and growing. Then I started aiming at adult audiences and I continued to get lead roles when I became older and looked older. So it's been a major part of my life, big time.

Sport and Being Bullied

When I was younger I played Gaelic football and a bit of basketball, but I was never really a soccer player as I wasn't that good. Gaelic football was my sport because nobody would get in my way! It was that type of thing: 'Get out of the way or I'll bust you!'

I was once in a holiday centre for this event called the Community Games. It must have been around midnight and I was sitting on a railing out on a balcony which was a bit wet. Next thing I knew my foot slipped and I fell back. Luckily, though, my foot caught in a clothes line which broke my fall. I fell head first, about two storeys, and I was knocked unconscious with a dislocated shoulder. Who knows what would have happened without that washing line!

I used to get bullied quite a bit when I was younger, from local people in the town. They just didn't like me for some reason or another. It started when I was about 12 and it finished when I was about 16. It stopped around then because I started going to the gym: I did bodybuilding for a year and nobody came near me after that. I was a lot bigger than I am now, as a result of that.

At the time it was like I'd come out of a disco and three or four guys would jump me for no reason whatsoever. I was at a carnival one night and there was one guy, he really, really aggravated me, he came up and smacked me for no reason whatsoever. Just stuff like that. I used to get black eyes, split lips or whatever, but never a broken nose. They used to always try and break my nose, but it never worked. That was the thing here, 'I'll break your f***ing snot!' I was never a fighter. But I decided to stand up for myself one day and I smacked one of them and they didn't come after me after that.

I still know these guys today. They've come up to me a few times since I've been home, since the band started out, saying, 'Congratulations, man', 'Sorry about all the *craic* when we were younger and all that' and I'm going, 'Yeah, yeah', just being nice about it and then I walk away, saying whatever. They were young and I was young. A few

of them are actually in jail now.

But it wasn't really in school where the fighting happened, that was the thing. It was outside school. The lads who did it were from a very bad part of town and were normally kicked out of school. There was one group of guys that just didn't like me and so they used to always bully me.

I do feel sympathy for younger lads growing up. But everybody had a bit of bullying in them as well – I used to pick on the quiet lads, and the louder lads used to pick on me. I didn't really pick on them; I used to have a laugh with the boys, giving them a hard time but I never hit someone for no reason.

The only time I actually started a fight was when my girlfriend was beaten up by two guys. It happened when we were coming out of a disco and she walked out in front of a car by accident, and this man got out and thumped her. So I wasn't very happy about that. I was 16 or 17, the disco was in my local community, it was like a youth club disco. I wasn't there when she was hit, but when I went up to her – her name was Yvonne and I went out with her for a year – I saw that her lip was split and it was bleeding. I went mad. It was a rush of blood to my head. He hit my girlfriend – you don't hit a girl, it's as simple as that. Those two lads didn't end up too well, you can imagine!

OPPOSITE PAGE: Kian at 14 with a cup which he won for stage performance
CENTRE: Kian and Shane in a school production of *Grease* (third and fourth from left)

How We Started

There were six of us originally in the band which has now led to Westlife, and we called it IOU. It was formed about two years ago. Five of us were The T Birds in *Grease*. Danny, Kenickie, Sonny, the five leather jacket boys in *Grease*. Mark wasn't actually one of the T Birds, he was Vince Fontaine. He was an amazing singer, that was the thing about Mark and that's how IOU started off.

The other lads were Michael Garret, Derek Lacey and Graham Keighron, and, of course, Shane. Graham is still one of my best mates, I haven't really seen the other two boys since.

When I originally met Graham around the age of 14 he was big into Metallica and bands like that, but he also loved Backstreet Boys and Take That, the same as me. As he always had the concerts on video. I used to sit down and watch the concerts with him and say, 'I want to do this, I want to get in front of that crowd of screaming girls and sing my heart out.' It was just something that gradually progressed through me. I still listen to Bon Jovi, Guns 'N Roses, all the stuff I used to listen to. And I listen to classical music, and rock music; I listen to George Michael for instance.

I think musically my family influenced me. When I was growing up there would be a violin playing in one room, a piano playing in another room, an electric guitar and a bass guitar. There was just this array of instruments coming out of the house.

We had actually bought tickets in Sligo to go and see Backstreet Boys play in the RDS in Dublin in March 1998. We got up at six o'clock in the morning, went down and queued for three hours. They are mainly a girls' band but we didn't care, we wanted to see the Backstreet Boys, because they were one of our favourite bands, it was just the way we were.

We used to do a lot of shows with around 16 songs in each set. It'd be like Take That songs, Boyzone songs, Backstreet Boys songs and then one or two of our own. We did a gig in the Quinnsworth car park in Sligo, a free open-air gig, and 2,000 people turned up.

We recorded two of our own songs and that's how we met up with Louis Walsh (the creator and manager of Boyzone). Shane's mum rang Louis and he put us on supporting the Backstreet Boys in the RDS in Dublin.

Shane and I had met him one night in Dublin and I can imagine when he heard the two songs he went, 'Hold on a second, these guys are good. I hear good voices in there.' Then he put us on supporting the Backstreet Boys and when he saw us onstage, it was, 'These guys are actually really good.'

You can imagine somebody queuing up for three hours to go and see a concert and then you end up meeting them, supporting them, hanging out with them, going to a club with them, playing basketball with them, as a band, it's just like you go from here to here in one day, it was just amazing.

Then Louis said he wasn't happy with one of the guys, as in 'that guy just doesn't look right'. That guy was Derek, so Derek was out of the picture. Then as time went on Louis felt that Graham didn't seem right, so that was Graham out of the picture. Then as time went on, when we met Nicky and Bryan, we decided to take a stand and said we wanted a band with just five vocalists. That would mean another guy going in order to bring in Nicky and Bryan. So Michael went.

There's a lot of heartache there. If I see them I say hello and that's really it. I can imagine it must be difficult for them, considering we've gone so far and they haven't. The only person who stuck beside us was Graham – the other two boys went their separate ways, which I can totally understand. I could never expect them to do anything else. Graham is still a very, very good friend of mine. He is still actually one of my two best friends outside the band. One of the other guys is now in college and the other guy is working. Graham has just applied for the army and it looks like he's going to get in. He's also a great soccer player and is playing football for a club in the north of Ireland.

We did have a female manager to start out with. She was the producer of all of the plays, but that was just a straight split through contracts, that had nothing to do with Louis at all.

It was amazing to get the support slot for Backstreet Boys, as we were huge fans. We came from a small town in the west of Ireland to be put in front of 10,000 screaming girls who loved boy bands, so you can imagine what it was like. When we walked out on stage and heard this wall of noise and screaming, it was unbelievable.

My mates all understood what I was doing. I did progress from rock to pop, but if you listen to some of the songs that we do now, there's a lot of rock guitar in them. Our very first number one single, 'Swear It Again', had a fair amount of rock guitar in it and some of the other ballads too. I love guitar music and a lot of our music is guitar sounding, but that wasn't the thing.

We then changed our name – because somebody else was called IOU – to Westside but had to change it to Westlife, because another band somewhere had the rights to that name too. We made damn sure nobody else was called Westlife – third time lucky!

Louis used to always says to me 'You're going to do it, you're going to do it', and I was going, 'Nah, we won't really, Louis' and he would say

'You will'. It was never reality to us. It's still not reality for me to sit here and say I've been in a band that's made a record by having a number one in the UK and Ireland with our first two singles, with 'Swear It Again' and 'If I Let You Go'.

That doesn't seem like reality to me, when I go back and think of what I wanted to do. The whole thing is like a dream and I'm waiting to wake up, that's the way I feel talking about what my life has been like so far.

Louis used always to say 'You're going to get a record deal, you're going to get this, you're going to get the other' and then the record companies came in and heard us singing. We sang nine songs live, acapella, in our showcase. We got rid of the music and there were the five of us, live mics, singing naked – well, you know what I mean! It sounded really good; we can sing. We stood there and sang for half an hour. Ten record companies came in and eight offered us a record deal. We didn't have a clue what was happening.

Ronan Gets Involved

We had supported the Backstreet Boys on the Sunday and we went up to Dublin on the Tuesday. I remember getting the train with Shane and Mark and a few of the other guys and walking out of Connolly railway station and I saw the front page of the *Evening Herald*. We were on the front page and page three, about us supporting the Backstreet Boys. I just said, 'Jesus Christ!'

I rolled it up and ran the whole way from Connolly station to the Clarence hotel. I ran into the room and screamed, 'Louis, Louis, Louis, did you see the paper?' Then I spotted Ronan and I went, 'Oh, my God, hiya Ronan.'

He had seen me running in and he was laughing and I could imagine him saying, 'Jesus, they're that fresh, they're running in with the paper to Louis.' I'm still like that, we're on the front cover of this and that. The whole thing is just amazing.

Ronan's involvement with us was a gradual thing. That meeting was in March 1998 and as time progressed he heard us sing, he helped us out with our singing and he got involved as a manager.

He started saying, 'Well, I think you should do this, I think you should do that, Louis, I think we should dress them like this.' He became artistically involved. Then, after a while, Louis said, 'You've been getting on really well with Ronan,' and we said, 'Yeah, yeah, he's great. He's helping us out an awful lot' and he said, 'How do you feel about him co-managing you with me? He can do the artistic side and I can do the business side,' and we were like, 'Yeah, definitely!' It was a big step. The experience that Ronan has – he's been on the road for six years, he's been in every country in the world, he's released a record in every country in the world.

Ronan knows the right thing to do, he knows the wrong thing to do and he can pass that on to us. He can help us develop as artists and try and keep us away from the bad side. The five lads in the band, we're the best of mates. I'd call over to Shane today, Mark might come in tonight. We might go and see a movie. We're like that. When we come home, we spend a lot of time together. Obviously we don't spend all our time together, but we still call into each other, give one another a ring: 'Do you want to go for a game of pitch and putt, a game of golf?'

You've got to understand. Mark, Shane and I have been best friends since we were kids and we know each other pretty well. When I go to Dublin I spend time with Bryan and Nicky and we go out together. We're best mates, it's as simple as that. We'll always be best mates. We're going to have little nitty gritty things now and again like 'Get your feet out of my face' at nine o'clock in the morning, when someone's in bad form and didn't go to bed until one o'clock.

Shane and myself usually share a room together, Bryan and Nicky stay in another and Mark has his own.

Work . . . and My Life as a Strippergram!

My first job was working in a clothes shop in Sligo, called EJ's Menswear. They're still very good friends of mine. I also worked in a shoe shop, Rogers and Lyons. I was 16 when I got that first job, during the summer. It was Monday to Saturday, 9 a.m. to 6 p.m. for £80 a week. It does put things in perspective, I was working a 40-hour week for 80 quid a week.

I always wanted to be in a band for my career. When I went to my career guidance teacher, I used to say, 'I want to do music' and 'I want to do performing arts in college', something that involved music, drama and dance, the three of them together. The jobs you could get out of that, you could be head of entertainment in Disneyland and things like that, so that's what I wanted to do.

They looked at my artistic side and said, 'Yeah, if that's what you really want to do'. I wanted to do what my brother did as well; go into music teaching. I was just about to begin teaching piano before the band

CLOCKWISE FROM LEFT: More autographs; Our first gold discs!; Kian drinking champagne after hearing of the band's record deal offers
OPPOSITE PAGE: The most important people of all – our fans

WESTLIFE in Our Own Words

1 4

started. I wanted to start teaching kids, so that I could improve as a teacher at the same time as helping kids to progress as piano players.

Then when I was younger I also started another little sideline – a strippergram! I was in a club and one of the girls who used to do all the musicals with me – she's about four or five years older than me – asked me if I knew what a kissogram was. I was like, 'Not really,' and she explained to me and said, 'Would you do one?' I looked at her and said, 'Yeah, I'll do one, for a laugh.' She said, 'You'd make good money from it, 50 or 60 quid.' I was 16. I said, 'Are you serious?' I used to go to the gym so I had quite a good body at the time – good pecs, good arms, and I agreed to do it.

Then I did the first one – all of the girl's friends thought I was really good, but I was a bit nervous. The routine was this: you'd go into a pub at ten o'clock on a Saturday night and they're all drunk going, 'Go onnnnn!' But it only takes two minutes. It was just a matter of reading a poem, pecking the girl on the

cheek and walking out. I had a pair of see-through trousers and a pair of little checked boxer shorts. I also had a dickie bow. I wore baby oil once.

I walked in like a Chippendale. I used to slick my hair back, like a real Chippendale guy, except obviously not big enough. So I used to walk in, bring the girl on to the stage, take the microphone off the band and read out the poem. It was mostly in the Adelaide pub in Sligo.

There were one or two strippergrams in Sligo at the time, but they were all old guys. They used to dress up as Tarzan and stuff like that and have their big bellies kind of hanging out, so I was the only young fellow. I did about six or seven of them. A lot of my mates used to come and watch just for a laugh, but I didn't care! It was a Saturday night out for me. After that, I'd go home, get changed. It would take me two minutes and I was out.

As time progressed and the band started and all that, I said, 'When I become famous they'll sell all my pictures.' It was quite funny, it was a really good laugh to be honest with you.

The Future and the Fans

Westlife has changed my life dramatically. I mean, obviously, you can imagine, I was working in a clothes shop and doing a normal everyday thing as an 18-year-old and then all of a sudden I was gone.

I left all my friends, all my family, everything I had behind me here, started off a new life in the pop industry. The stuff we've learned as a band is just amazing, the way our lives have changed. We've been to nearly every part of Ireland and Britain and lots of other countries at this stage. It doesn't get any better than this.

I do like splashing out on designer clothes. I spend so much money on clothes now, it's unbelievable. I would never have spent £100 on a jumper before. I'm just so fashion-conscious now, if I can afford to buy something.

I got a car recently; I bought a Ford Fiesta off my sister to learn how to drive. I'd had a few driving lessons to learn the basics. I got into the car and put it into reverse but I was so excited that zas I was reversing out I smashed into a wall!

Our fans are absolutely fantastic. We've met a lot of fans around the world and we treat them just the same as any other people. A

always say, 'Yeah.' Love is blind, you never know who you're going to fall in love with. Just because they like our music doesn't make them any different to me.

Some of the fans can get quite crazy sometimes, but you can understand that, they're excited and they see a band. As I say, to me it's not realistic. We're number one with the first two singles, so it's not realistic for me to say why they like us as a band or why they like me as a person because they see us in this band and they want to meet us, they want photographs, autographs. That's all fine, that's all nice and relaxed. But when we go out to Asia and places like that, it's different, that's

pull your hair and try and grab your jewellery, which has happened to me. I've had two really good rings pulled off me, like when I've put my hand down into the audience.

I don't know why I'm made out to be this sex symbol. My hair is originally brown, I've been dyeing it blond since I was 14 and I prefer it to be blond. I think we're all, as individuals, very, very popular. The band is a popular band. If you look at the *Smash Hits* poll, we had one single out and all five of us were in the top 30. I was number 2, Shane was 10, Bryan was 17 . . . If you look at it like that, it's just amazing the way we've jumped in so soon, but if people tell me that I'm the most

popular I say, 'Well, I'm not the most popular,' because I'm not. There have been loads of different polls. I might have won one, Shane might have won one. Bryan, Mark, Nicky, everybody's won a poll. So I think everybody's just as popular as everybody else.

My main ambition for the band? I want this band to become the biggest boy band that have ever lived. I want to kick the Backstreet Boys' asses. They've sold 37 million albums world-wide and I want to sell 60 million. Just to beat them. That's my goal.

Of course, if you ask a footballer who they want to be, they want to be Pelé. That's the way we look at it. We've got to aim as high as we can and that's what we're doing. We're aiming to the highest heights. We want to be the male Spice Girls.

I can see myself living in Sligo, buying a house, putting my family in a house and visiting all the time. This is the place I'll always consider to be home. I'd like to live in Sydney for a while, though, it's beautiful. And I'd like to explore a bit. I'm only 19. God, what I've accomplished for a 19-year-old is a hell of a lot, a hell of lot.

I'd like to do a bit of acting when this all finishes. I'd love to move on. Whatever the band's life is, nobody can ever say, it could be five years, we could do a Bee Gees on it, you never know. I'd like to do TV presenting; we've presented TV shows four times now. I really like that, I think it's great.

I'd also love to do a solo record, there are just so many things that I'd love to do. We're treated absolutely fantastically in Sligo. There's still the odd one or two begrudgers who'll roar at us and say 'Nice to meet you, thanks very much' and just walk away. You never satisfy them. You never give them stick back, because that's what they're looking for.

Apart from that, Sligo is a fantastic place and people treat us very, very well. We're delighted that we're from here. Only the people from Sligo, including the shops like the Record Room and Star Records, supported us from the start and if it wasn't for them we wouldn't be here.

Shane Filan

Family

I grew up in the centre of Sligo town. I was brought up above a restaurant, which my family owns and runs. My mum is originally from Kiltimagh in Co. Mayo which is the same small town that Boyzone manager Louis Walsh is from.

I have three brothers and three sisters, all older than me. I'm the youngest, the baby of the family. The oldest is Finbar, who is 31 and an industrial engineer. He lives near Sligo as well. Peter is 30; he's a doctor in Dublin. Then there's Yvonne, she's 28 and she's a secondary school teacher in Sligo. Liam is 27 and he's the horseman of the family – my family are very big into horses. Liam is a qualified accountant, he went to college to do it, but has decided to work with horses as his career.

After Liam is Denise. She is 24 and she works as a physiotherapist in Dublin. Then there's Mairead, who is 22. She's working for Bus Eireann, the bus company, in Dublin. She does marketing for them.

Finbar is married, as is Peter; Finbar has two kids and Peter has one. I'm the godfather of Finbar's first child, Killian. He's very special to me, because being a godfather is a cool thing. I'm very close to him. He's only four but he's getting into singing now. He's always watching telly, sitting in front of it with his microphone.

I have to admit that when I was growing up I did get spoiled because I was the youngest. I was looked after until I matured. I got whatever I wanted. Then, when I got a bit older, everybody was the same really. But when I was younger, definitely I was spoiled rotten.

I had three big brothers all my life, so nobody would mess with me when I was younger, which was brilliant. But it was good growing up in a big family, because you had a variety of siblings; if you had an argument with one you had five others to go and cry to.

My dad's name is Peter and my mother's name is

Mae. They run a restaurant in Sligo. My dad was always a singer, a big Jim Reeves fan. He was the only singer in the family. I got my singing from my dad, definitely, passed on in my genes.

It was deadly growing up over a restaurant: you always had a meal within five seconds and it is based in the centre of town. Everything is close by – a sports shop, video shop. I'm glad I grew up in a restaurant.

I have been into horses all my life, as have my whole family. I've a load of trophies from show-jumping. Then I started getting into singing when I was about 12 or 13. I loved Michael Jackson when I was younger – I was a Michael Jackson fanatic. When I was about 13 I decided to start singing and I did a play. But before that it was more or less the usual – sport.

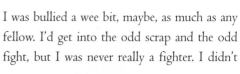

School

The first school I went to was Scoil Fatima in Sligo. It was a primary school and I spent four years there from the age of four up to second class.

I remember my first day at school well because I remember my mother leaving me there. Then my brother, Finbar, came up and he was at the window making faces and slagging me and there was me bawling my eyes out. I will never forget it; it was a horrible day. I think Miss Sheehan was my first teacher and then I went to St John's, because it was a bigger school.

I loved football – soccer and Gaelic. I was really into it. I was never top class or anything but I just loved playing football when I was younger and then Michael Jackson took over for about three or four years when I was eight or nine.

I did everything he did, including the moonwalk. I can still do the moonwalk and I often do it when we're on TV now. I had all his records, all the videos. I used to spend hours watching them.

Then I went to secondary school, Summerhill College. It's a huge school and has about 1,200 pupils – all boys – and 50 or 60 teachers. The headmaster is a priest. They basically helped me to where I am now; they got me into musicals and we did a lot of school plays.

It was a bit weird to go to Summerhill at first. You had all the big boys, who were 18, there, and here was me coming in at the age of 12 and about two feet tall. It was different because I was used to having my own age group around me and then I was into a big stretch and I hoped that I would settle down.

I remember my first day at Summerhill. There is a big hill going up to the college and I used to walk from the restaurant. I remember having a huge bag of books – you could have put three TVs in it. It was killing me.

I had to take 15 books, being the first day at school. Everyone was laughing at me because of the size of the bag; the bag was almost bigger than I was. I was tiny when I was 12: I was definitely the smallest thing you'd ever see for a 12-year-old.

I didn't really get bullied in secondary school I got slagged for singing and because I was small

I was bullied a wee bit, maybe, as much as any fellow. I'd get into the odd scrap and the odd fight, but I was never really a fighter. I didn't fight that much in school. A couple of times I'd get into a ruck, but I was never bullied and I never bullied others. Summerhill was grand, though; it opened my eyes to everything and gave me great opportunities.

I was a year ahead of Kian. Mark was in Kian's year and I was a year ahead of the two of them. I knew Kian around that time really well. I'd known him before but we got to be really good mates when we started doing plays together and then Mark came in when I was about 15, so I got friendly with him.

I liked accountancy a lot. I got an A with honours in my Leaving Cert. I hated science. I couldn't fathom that at all. My best subject was English and I was good at maths, chemistry and business organisation.

I liked school, but I didn't love it. I did my homework, got good grades, but I wasn't a genius. I never wanted to be a doctor or anything like that. So accountancy was what I wanted to do, but not what I'd have loved to do – singing is what I really wanted to do. I just got lucky.

I went to college for six months after school, where I studied marketing and accountancy. But I wasn't really happy in the college – Limerick Regional College – it wasn't exactly what I wanted to do.

Then the band started getting better and better – we were meeting Louis at the time – and I made the decision to leave college, although I could have got back in the following year to do total accountancy.

Sport

Nearly everybody in Summerhill played Gaelic football or soccer, but I was more into rugby. I wasn't really good enough to be on the school Gaelic football team but I did enjoy soccer, although I never took it as seriously as singing. I was into rugby in a big way when I was 15 or 16 and stopped singing for about a year to play rugby for Connacht. The singing took over later, when the band was getting together.

I started playing rugby when I was younger, but not seriously until I joined Sligo RFC. My brothers were big into rugby, they played for Ireland schools and college teams and Connacht teams, though it began to take up too much time for Liam as he wanted to concentrate on the horses. Finbar played rugby as well, so it was a natural thing for me to do. I loved it, I played outside-half, number ten.

TOP: Peter's wedding. From left: Mairead, Shane, Denise, Liam, Mam, Peter, Ciara, Dad,
Yvonne, Killian, Finbar, Geraldine
BOTTOM: Shane on his confirmation day

Summerhill wasn't a big rugby school, so when I did training in school I was usually left to myself with my own teacher, who also liked rugby. The club itself wasn't very big, it was second and third division, but when we went to Connacht, that was top level.

I had a few injuries. I injured my shoulder when I chipped my shoulder blade during a rugby game. But I've never stayed a night in a hospital, except when I was born. It was just the usual, tetanus injections after banging my head or something like that.

I also won trophies for kick-boxing. I did it for two years, when I was 10 or 11, just something to do during the week, and then I started to like it. I'm not that good at it anymore, but I still throw a few kicks if any fellow starts on me, you know.

Work

I got my first job when I was 16. I worked across the road from the restaurant for a couple of days in a hardware store and then I worked in EJ's Menswear for a couple of days at Christmas. Kian worked there as well. After that I had another job for about four months, just as the band was starting, when I needed some money for myself. That was in Buckley's. It is a builders' provider's store, it's got bricks and wood and stuff like that. That was the only serious job I really had.

I was fairly well paid there, which was good but you have to work hard. The first month I was getting £220 because I wasn't on full taxes, but I got a bit less, maybe £200, after that.

How We Met

I started singing Billy Joel's 'Uptown Girl' when I was very young. I used to love singing and I was a very good singer when I was young. It's my life, singing, it was the best thing I could do. But it was Michael Jackson who encouraged me to go on stage; I got a lot of inspiration from him.

I was never a mad record buyer, I always used to wonder why people would buy stuff rather than tape it off the radio. I bought Michael Jackson because I loved him, but even after Michael Jackson, when I was 12, 13, 14, I was going, 'Hey, why are you buying these records, you can listen to this on the radio? I can tape it.' But when I was younger I liked

Billy Joel. My mum used to get all the records, 'Uptown Girl' and all that, when I was really young.

When Boyzone came out, I bought a lot of Boyzone singles and albums. I didn't buy every single; I wasn't a fanatical Boyzone fan. I know a lot of lads my age might have laughed at them but I was jealous as hell

of them, I respected them. I was nearly afraid going into record shops buying Boyzone records, people would look at you and think, 'What are you buying one of them for?' Seriously, back then it wasn't cool. Like, Take That were huge, but it wasn't cool to go to a Take That concert. People would look at you and go, 'What a weirdo.' Now, everybody goes to Boyzone concerts.

It's the whole lifestyle of boy bands – we are a boy band. But it's changed, it's not just little girls anymore, it's women, it's men, it's everybody that goes to see bands and buys records. If you've a good song your music is respected, that's the way it is.

It's not all about showing off six packs and that kind of stuff anymore; that's not what we're about. We're big into singing and we're big into our performance and that's what we portray most. Back then, that was what you did, you did all that, shaking the six packs.

So when I started acting in plays at school, that was my thing, that was what I was happy doing. I used to do plays in the local theatre, the Hawkswell, so I did different plays with different production companies from Sligo. We did maybe two a year, one around February or March and another at Christmas. So that went on for four or five years.

In school, David McEvoy was the teacher in charge of us for the musicals while a local production company in Sligo used also to be involved.

It was the same plays, *Grease* and *Oliver*. I did *Grease* about four times and it was the first play I did. We also did *Annie Get Your Gun*.

The six original members of IOU started off in *Grease*. The six of us used to sing Backstreet Boys songs in the middle of *Grease*. At the beginning it was a joke, it was a laugh, just for the *craic*, then we did another gig, and another gig, then eventually people started saying, 'They're good, they're good singers.'

The name IOU was just picked for us. It actually came from a fellow that owns a sandwich shop over the road; he did voice coaching with us, and he was also into plays himself. He wrote down a load of names and we picked IOU, saying it was the best one.

We recorded three songs ourselves on to a CD. They included a song called 'Together Forever', which Mark and I wrote, and 'Everlasting Love', a song Mark wrote. They weren't great songs, but they were good for us. We also did a song called 'Pinball Wizard' by The Who.

My mother thought, as she was from Kiltimagh, Louis Walsh's home

town, that she'd be able to get him interested in us. She rang Louis for ages, but couldn't get him. She knew that Louis was probably the best manager in pop and still is. She just wanted somebody to look after us and because she was from Kiltimagh she felt that Louis might listen to her, although she knew he was a busy man. She knew him when she was younger. Her family knew his family really well, although they probably hadn't spoken to each other for 20, 30 years.

Eventually she managed to talk to him. I was up at my sister's house for her friend's 21st and I remember my mum rang and she said, 'I was

ringing him, in my sister's house, so I could get total silence. He answered and he went, 'How are you doing, Shane, how are you keeping? Come over to the Pod. I'll be there tonight, about half eleven.' I remember he said he was bringing along Dani Behr, because Dani Behr was in town. I was going, 'Dani Behr's going to be there.' I was dying to see Louis and I was dying to see Dani Behr as well. I went in and told Kian and he wouldn't believe me. So we went up to Dublin. Louis had said he'd be waiting for us at half eleven at the Chocolate Bar [which is part of the Pod nightclub].

talking to Louis Walsh.' I wouldn't believe her, and she rang back three times and I still wouldn't believe her. I was saying, 'Will you stop talking rubbish? What are you talking about?' She just laughed and said, 'He's been on the phone.'

So I rang him. I was so nervous ringing. I remember I was in the toilet

We went in and were taken upstairs to the VIP section. There was nobody there but Louis and ourselves. So we sat down and we showed him the CD and he said, 'I saw you on the telly and your mum rang and told me all about you and she is so chuffed.'

He had already seen us as IOU on a TV show we'd done at Christmas, called *Nationwide*. We had appeared because we'd visited a local hospital and sang to the patients. That was our first appearance on TV.

He said straightaway, 'I can't manage you, but I can help you.' So in a way I was kind of devastated but we were happy he was going to help us out. He looked at the cover of the CD and said, 'Six is too many.' At that stage I didn't care, I just wanted him to manage us. Full stop. We wanted Louis Walsh to be our manager.

As we were leaving he said he'd put us on with Boyzone in The Point

keeping? How are you doing?' and invited me to Ronan's 21st. So Michael, one of the fellows that used to be in the band, and myself went up and it was deadly.

It felt like I was going to a World Music Awards or something. I was so young, so nervous, I didn't know what to wear, I didn't know what to do. I went and I still didn't think my name would be on the list. So I said my name and they had to look down about 15 pages before they finally found it. I got to meet Ronan at the party. He came by me and I put out my hand, shook his hand and said, 'Happy birthday, Ronan.' He

that Christmas and we went, 'Oh, my God, we're playing the Point Depot with Boyzone!' So we went home and I said to the boys, 'I met Louis last night,' and they were all chuffed. I told them he'd said 'Six is too many' and that any one of us could be asked to leave.

Louis rang me about two days later and just said, 'How are you

said, 'Thanks a lot,' but he didn't know who we were, obviously. Eventually, Louis pointed out who we were and formally introduced us. After that Louis got more and more interested in us. We sent him a video and I kept pestering him really, just to say hello. Every time I got off the phone, I was thinking, 'Will he ever talk to this band again, he's got Boyzone, he doesn't need another band, will he just go and leave us?' because he wasn't our manager, he was just helping us out and that's the way it was. So every time I was going 'Will I talk to you soon?' he was saying, 'Yeah, I'll give you a ring.' So that's the way it was, Louis would ring me whenever. He rang me every few days and about two weeks later he said, 'You're supporting the Backstreet Boys.'

We didn't know what to do or say. We had nothing prepared, we only had about two songs which we wrote ourselves. So we were being thrown into the lion's den, getting up on stage with the Backstreet Boys, and doing our own little thing, jumping around like lunatics. Then we got to meet the Backstreet Boys, played basketball all day with them. It was just the best two days of my life.

Straight after that Louis got really interested in us. He had seen the reaction of the crowd, who were great. He was saying, 'I can't manage you, but I can't let go of you either, I have to manage you, I want to be your manager.' He was kind of saying, 'Do you want me to be your manager?' We were delighted and we jumped at it.

Almost immediately Derek had to leave the band. That was hard, because he was my best friend at the time and I had to tell him. Then Graham had to go, and Graham was, and still is, a really good friend of ours. Michael was the last to go.

It was unfortunate. Six was probably too many, anyway. It was just a shame that Louis didn't think they suited the group. What it really came down to was either we give up the opportunity of a lifetime and stick by the other three lads to continue with IOU or we go for it with Louis Walsh as our manager. We couldn't turn that down, it was the chance of a lifetime. But it was unfortunate it was those three guys; it could have been any of us. We're

just lucky it wasn't, thanks be to God, it's just the way it went.

I'd known Graham and Derek all my life and it was really hard letting them go. If I see the lads on the street we'll say hello and talk to each other. They don't call us, but I can hardly blame them. It was their dream as much as it was ours and then they see us being successful; your heart goes out to them. I have a lot of respect for Graham still, because he does talk to me, but that's basically how things go. Nicky and Bryan came in through the auditions after that.

We then had eight record companies offering us deals. A couple more came to see us but I didn't think they were interested in us. The RCA/BMG offer was definitely the best.

Simon Cowell, A&R man with BMG, became involved with us. At that stage Five were really big and we were really small, so he told us exactly what he wanted to do, how we felt about it and what he'd like us to do. He was just telling us our dream. I could see all my dreams coming through. We all jumped at it and Louis said, 'What do you think?' and we said, 'We love it.' So Louis said to us, 'This is the man for us, this is the record company for us.' It just hit off after that.

We did a lot of recording in Sweden, with Andres Bagge. I had never been outside Ireland or Britain before. It was a major culture shock to land in Sweden. I saw all this snow; it was like going to another planet. You see all these places on maps but you never expect it, I was ringing all my mates saying, 'I'm in Sweden!' It was a weird thing. Now, it doesn't matter where I land, Singapore, Thailand, it's like 'Oh, yeah, next airport', if you know what I mean. We went to the Far East, Australia and New Zealand – every country, you name it, we've been in it, for most of 1999.

I had never been in a band before; my first

...and was TOU. Kian was the one who was big into bands. It is and it isn't unusual for lads of our age to be into that type of music, but it's unusual for a band like us to be doing so well. You wouldn't think three of us are from a town that's in the west of Ireland, you'd think 'they must be from Dublin', because that's where everyone thinks the opportunities are.

But we just went out and did it and we got lucky. There's loads of other blokes my age or younger than me, in other country towns, that might get a chance as well. The fact that you're not from Dublin means that you mightn't get as much of a chance, because there aren't as many schools, or as much drama, or theatre. You'd never think it, but that's the way it is. There are people like me everywhere, they just need to get more of a chance. But we got lucky.

The Future

It's brilliant to go home to Sligo; we don't get home that often. We were at a reception in Sligo recently when the mayor gave us the keys of the town and it was brilliant to have our families, cousins, everybody there – the whole town was out to see us.

But you get begrudgers everywhere. I've not had a fellow trying to start on me yet, to be honest with you. A couple of fellows have given me dodgy eyes and stuff, but we're not back in Ireland that much, although we are recognised here and in England now.

I don't think the band has changed me as a person. It just changes your outlook on life; you get to wear nicer clothes, you get to go to cool places, you get to see the world.

But in a way, I don't think money will change me as a person: I don't think I'll become arrogant. A lot of people do, so you have to be careful, you just have to make sure

you have your family to keep you on the ground. I don't think I'm that kind of person, I don't think any of us are. We all come from nice homes and we've all been taught well.

I got a car last October (1998), a BMW. I've been driving since my 17th birthday when I got my licence: I was so excited to get it. I've never had a scrape in my car, although I've had a few hubcaps scraped while parking.

We're not pop stars yet but we're doing well. I can't see myself as a pop star. I look on Michael Jackson as a pop star, Madonna as a pop star, but not me. Mark and I would love to meet Michael Jackson, that's our big ambition.

It's a privilege when people know you, call to your house, but sometimes you want to be alone to talk to your mum and dad, and you have to literally lock yourself away from everything because your phone will ring or something will happen.

I hope that, in a year's time, if the band keeps doing well, my family will build a house, because we have a lot of land just outside town and we already have a site for a house. So we hope to move out there, but it's going to be weird, moving a mile outside town. It will be strange going to a fridge to get a drink instead of grabbing a can of Coke off the shelf downstairs. It will be different.

I like Sligo a lot. It's busy for a small town yet quiet compared to somewhere like Dublin. But it's got everything in it, it's cool to come home to.

Mark Feehily

Family

I grew up with my family in a townland about two miles outside Sligo town. I've got two brothers and I'm the eldest. The next eldest to me is Barry. He is aged 14 and is still at school. He is going into third year. Then there's Colin. He has just turned ten. I have no sisters; it has always been us three boys.

Every little place in the world has its own little problems that young people have to deal with but where we live in Sligo it's a pretty quiet place and not that much happens.

My brothers are kind of pretty young so they haven't really got involved with girls yet, especially the younger one. All he cares about is football, and the second one, I'm sure he's starting to get into girls and everything now, but I don't think he's got to the stage where he needs advice or anything yet!

Apart from that, we were always very close to our parents – they were always the first people we'd turn to. So, there's not much my two brothers would come to me for advice for, but if they did need some they'd call me up. Though it's rarely, rarely happened. As they're pretty young they haven't really come across any major problems – they're young and carefree.

My mum's name is Marie and my dad's name is Oliver. My mum is a housewife and she also works in the civil service in Sligo. She's based in government buildings where she works for the Department of Agriculture and Food. Dad has been very successful for the past 15 years or so running his own business. He used to be the Sligo agent for Senator windows but he recently stopped doing windows and he just does conservatories now.

Dad is from the outskirts of Sligo town and my mum is from Sligo town itself. We used to live two miles outside the town, a really small area. It was very close to town, but it wasn't like *The Waltons* or anything, it was just slightly different in that I used to go next door to my cousin's house or even to my granny's house as opposed to maybe going to the bowling alley or stuff like that.

There were some farms around. My grandfather had a small farm and I used to help him out every now and again during the summer. He only lived over the road from me, but I didn't come from a farming family or anything like that.

School – and Religion

I was actually in a school outside town for primary school. It was called St Patrick's National School. I can't really remember my first day but I can remember a lot of days throughout.

I always got on pretty well with my teachers, I don't know if I ever had a favourite or a least favourite. There were actually two teachers in particular that started the ball rolling to a certain degree when it comes to music. There was one teacher called Padraig Foran and he was the headmaster of the school. He used to lead the choir at the parish church, with which I sang. We might practise one night a week in the church for mass on Sundays and then we'd have a little choir in school, just for fun really.

Then there was another guy called Pat Stenson, he actually became headmaster after Padraig Foran left and he directed the first musical that I did. It was a very small affair. There were only about 32 people in my class and we just put it on as a class for all the other classes. It was very small scale, but I suppose it was the first thing I ever did. I did the usual Christmas nativity plays, but the first one I remember doing was one called *Scrooged*, which was loosely based on Scrooge.

I then went to Summerhill College for secondary school – where Kian and Shane also went. I found it a big difference from primary school. Basically, the school that I had gone to previously had about 330 people compared to over a thousand in Summerhill. In Summerhill there are two massive buildings with a huge swimming-pool and gym. It was absolutely enormous compared to the school I used to go to and I didn't know what to think of it at first, even though there wasn't much difference between the people who lived outside the town and those from inside the town.

There wasn't much for me to do where I lived – I used to hang around with my cousins and watch TV and play a few computer games. But for the people who lived in the town, there were a lot more young people their age living around them. They could go into the town centre and their parents wouldn't worry about them as much as my parents worried about me going into town, because it was further away or whatever. Basically I'd say the townspeople would have been slightly more mature than people who lived outside the town for the simple reason that they lived in the town, if you know what I mean. It was just kind of weird because all the people in my new class were all saying things like, 'Oh, we went out to this disco at the weekend' and 'What did you think of it?' and 'Was it good?' and all this, while I hadn't been to a disco in my life before.

When I started in Summerhill, the subjects I picked were English, Irish, maths and then French, business studies and woodwork, as well as science and geography. I didn't like French at all at the start. I just couldn't get into it until the end of second year, going into third year, when I went to France on a school exchange that my French teacher organised. A good few pupils from the school went. I don't know what happened to me there but I came back from France loving French. I think I'm more the type of person that could learn a language like French by actually going there and speaking it rather than learning it from a book.

I could have a conversation now in French with somebody if the person talked slowly or whatever. I'm not fluent or anything, but I know a little bit of French. We went to Paris with the band recently and we invited the press to a lunch. I tried to speak a little French but I'm not too forward about speaking it.

In my Junior Cert, my strongest subjects turned out to be woodwork, science and French, I was happy enough at that. When I was coming up to my Leaving Cert, I was always thinking of this, that and the other of what I'd do, but I always knew at the bottom of my heart and inside my head that I would try and make some sort of music career. So it's kind of weird the way it worked out.

At school I didn't get bullied at all, really. Obviously, it took me a little bit of time to get to know people, but it wasn't too long before I got to make new friends. My best friend, Rowan, comes from town. I've known him since I was very young and that kind of helped me as well because I got to know a lot of people from his old class too. I just got to know him from being in town. We were always interested in music in a big, big way.

When I got into secondary school and I got to know all the other lads, I'd hear about the discos that would be on at the weekend. After another year or two I started going out to discos and then eventually when I got old enough to get in – even though I wasn't 18 but I looked old enough to get in – I used to go to the nightclubs in Sligo. Basically, I gradually started getting into going to discos and meeting girls, hanging about and having a good laugh.

I'm afraid I broke my Confirmation pledge, which meant I took a drink before I turned 18. I obviously knew right from wrong, but I'm not the type of person that would jump into a fire if everyone else did. I'd make my own decisions. Now at this point in my life I wouldn't make a pledge to God if I wasn't going to keep it, but I didn't understand it then and everyone else in my class was doing it, so I did it too.

I am a religious person. I pray every single night without fail. I think it's very important. Personally I was brought up in a Catholic family and I went to mass every Sunday with my parents and we prayed in school before lunch and everything like that, just like an average young Irish Catholic fellow's lifestyle. But ever since I got into the band and growing up, maybe from my Junior Cert and Leaving Cert, I've kind of got into really praying to God. It does disappoint me that more young people have stopped going to Mass. I'm very,

very glad that my parents took me to Mass each Sunday: it is something in my life that I don't regret at all.

Obviously, I spend a lot of time outside Ireland now and especially in London and it's very hard to find a Catholic church around. I'm sure there's loads of them but how would I go about starting to find them? Anyway, a lot of the time we're working all day Sunday, but everytime I do get a chance I go to Mass. Priests run Summerhill but I was never tempted to become a priest. I don't think that would be my sort of life. With all due respect to priests, and fair play to them, personally I never even thought about becoming a priest. I always definitely wanted to get married and I always wanted to grow up having girlfriends. I do think priests should be allowed to get married because I think there'd be a lot more priests if that were the case. It's obviously natural for me to like women or whatever – I suppose it

is the '90s – it's natural for people to like the opposite sex.

But if they want to be a priest and the only thing holding them back is that they don't want to give up women, so to speak, then I think that's really, really sad and it shouldn't affect them being a priest at all.

Sport

There's a tennis club about five miles from my house and my dad used to play a lot of squash there. When I was younger, if my mum was in town or if there wasn't anybody in the house to mind me, he'd take me down if there was a squash match.

Then I actually got into it and I used to ask him – even if there was somebody in the house – if I could go with him anyway and, gradually, when he was having a break in the middle of a game, I used to go on and play a bit.

I started to play badminton and tennis and then I got into squash after that. I basically lived for it for a few years. I spent all of my time playing tennis during the summer and at weekends and I got really, really into it.

I used to travel all over Ireland playing tennis tournaments and I even got on to the Connacht tennis team and played at

LEFT: Mark on his confirmation day with his mam, dad and brothers, Barry and Colin
RIGHT: Seven-year-old Mark on his communion day

inter-provincial level. I just really, really enjoyed it. Then I got a job in Sligo and I didn't have as much time for it, because I wanted to have a bit of money for myself, rather than getting money off my parents the whole time. I don't think I was good enough to be Ireland's answer to Tim Henman, but I definitely enjoyed it.

I used to watch Wimbledon every year without fail. The first real match I can remember watching was when Steffi Graf and Martina Navratilova were playing the Wimbledon final. I got into tennis when Stefan Edberg, Boris Becker and John McEnroe were around.

I also played soccer and in primary school I played Gaelic football. Soccer is a big, big thing in Sligo. I used to play all the time in school and over at my friend's house or wherever. When I got on to the local football team I played midfield. I suppose I would have classed myself as quite a sporty person. We don't get much opportunity now, but if I had the chance I would definitely play sport.

Work

My very first job was working in the kitchen of a small restaurant called Café Yeats in Sligo [named after W.B. Yeats, the most famous poet from Ireland, who is buried near Sligo]. It was just basically cleaning up. I was about 15.

I can remember getting my first pay packet. It was really weird as I was so chuffed with myself; I couldn't believe that I was getting paid after doing a week's work. You know the way you look at your parents all grown up and they get paid every week, when they do a week's work.

All of a sudden I didn't need to go and ask my mum if I could have money to go into town on a Saturday anymore because I'd my own money. It wasn't a massive wage, but it was like a thousand pounds to me. I think I spent it on total crap, it probably dwindled away before I knew it, knowing me. I think I went out for drinks, the cinema, whatever.

Then I worked in Staunton's sports shop in Sligo for four to six months. After that I worked in my auntie's photographic shop in Sligo. I also worked in Burger King for a while but I used to absolutely hate that. I would start work at about 8 p.m. in the evening. The place would close at 1 a.m. or 2 a.m., but then you had to take all the machinery apart to clean it. Nobody knew how to do it properly because the restaurant had only recently opened, so we were there until five in the morning cleaning up. I do think, sometimes, when I go somewhere like Burger King today that I could

still be working in a place like that.

Everyone can see the lifestyle that I live – obviously it has many bonuses and advantages to it – but when I worked in Burger King, at the end of the day I was working and I was getting paid for it, and I never think, 'Oh, imagine if that was me now. God, it would be hell.'

In certain ways I miss having a totally average lifestyle, because I really, really loved it and I miss working in some place like a shop or Burger King, and having money to go out for a few drinks with your mates or whatever, because I don't get to do that anymore.

How We Met

My grandparents on my mum's side of the family always used to enter my mum and her sisters and brother into the *Feis* and poetry competitions. They enjoyed singing and reciting poems and one or two of my cousins were very good at it. My mum and one of my aunts in particular, used to go to see musicals and they would take all of their children with them.

I'd never considered a career in music until I went to see musicals and all of a sudden I started to get a shiver up my spine for whatever musical I went to. It was like, 'Oh, my God, I want to be on that stage so much it's unbelievable.' Coming out of the front doors of the theatre I would think, 'How am I going to get into it?' I didn't have the first idea about how to get into a musical and that's probably what inspired me to do it so much. I basically started singing because I used to love the film *Grease.* I got a video of it off a cousin and I used to watch it 25 times a day, morning, noon and night.

The first album I ever got, from Santa Claus one Christmas, was Michael Jackson's *Bad*. The first song I ever bought, I think, was 'Uptown Girl' by Billy Joel. I never really bought that many singles, I don't know why. Now that I'm in the business, I ask myself if I was a real Michael Jackson fan when I didn't go and buy the singles. I suppose I was; you don't have to buy the singles to be a fan – you just have to like the music.

Although I didn't buy many singles, I still loved music and I used to look around in the Record Room after school. I didn't know Kian and Shane that well at school, at first. Shane was the year ahead of me and Kian was in the same year but in a totally different class. I'm sure I bumped into them in the corridors without knowing who they were but I didn't get to know them properly until *Grease*.

The very first *Grease* we were in, I would have been about 16. The person who put it together was a music teacher called David McEvoy. He played a big part in getting me involved because, as I came from outside town, I was always a very shy person. I didn't have much confidence when it came to performing, so when I was asked to sing at auditions I wouldn't have given it my all, because I would have been so nervous at the time. Mr McEvoy encouraged me and helped me gain some confidence.

I wasn't very musical at the time because, unfortunately, there were no music classes in my school unless you stayed after school and I always wanted to get home because I was tired. But Mr McEvoy made me a lot more at ease with myself.

I have absolutely no idea where my voice, as in my talent, comes from nor where my musical interests come from: I'm really into R&B and that's hardly a traditional kind of Irish music. I never once got voice coaching

before the band but we recently had a lesson with a guy called David Laudup who trains the Spice Girls. He came in for an hour one day to teach us how to warm our voices up because they were starting to get strained: we were singing so much and we didn't know how to warm them up properly, so we were hurting our voices. But that's the only voice training I've had. It all just happened naturally, really.

I was 18 when we got the record deal signed. That was one of the biggest days of my life. We had just come off the Boyzone tour and we were called back over to London about four days later to sign the contract. The whole way was like, 'I can't believe this is happening.' It was such a brilliant feeling.

I didn't go out celebrating that night because, as I'm such a family man and I'm really close to all my friends back home, I obviously wanted to celebrate with my family. But, unfortunately, we signed the record deal in the evening and we couldn't get a flight out, so we had to wait until the next day before we could get home. We just went back to the hotel and had a drink or two – we were all trying to save our energy to celebrate when we got back to Sligo.

It was like a big, big shock. We were basically thrown in at the deep end with the Boyzone tour in September 1998. Coming from Sligo, even though it's a big town, it's quite average and there's nothing out of the ordinary that happens there. For me to suddenly be travelling around with a very famous group of people – Boyzone – and to be travelling all over England, a place I'd only been once or twice before, for three and a half weeks, was really exciting.

It was just like changing from really cold water to really hot water, a total change in lifestyle over the space of basically the flight from Ireland to England, and to tell you the truth it scared me. I was a real home type person. Although I used to play a lot of tennis in other parts of Ireland, and would be away from home for say a week every month or month and a half, I was pretty much a homeboy, so to speak. From spending most of my time at home, either in the house or in a mate's house, all of a sudden I was in a bus travelling the whole of the UK, going on stage in front of thousands of people every single night, and spending quite a bit of time with Ronan and the lads from Boyzone.

I didn't know what hit me: I was away from home every night at that stage, unfortunately, we didn't have our sponsorship for free mobile phone bills, so I was very, very wary of making phone calls and obviously the band was starting off. We're not millionaires – far from it – but we've made a little bit of money now so we can afford to make a few phone calls here and there. Back then, though, it was the very start of the band and I was wary of making phone calls all the way from England to Ireland, so I was basically homesick for the first long time.

I still get homesick but I've learned to deal with it now – I know I have to cope with it, and thank God for the sponsorship we get from Esat. If it wasn't for that I don't know where I'd be, because I'd be spending all my money on phone calls! It was just a total change of lifestyle; it was going from an average Sligo boy's lifestyle to the lifestyle of someone in a boy band, which is a lot different, let me tell you.

When 'Swear It Again' went to number one, we were in PWL and we were all sitting around the table with our phones lined up, waiting for a phone call. Pete Waterman, who we recorded three or four songs with, was there and he brought down a bottle of champagne for us and popped it and we all kind of just jumped around the room like raving lunatics for ages.

The way it is with instruments in the band is that Kian is pretty handy on piano and guitar. Bryan plays a little bit of piano and guitar as well. Myself, I have a good ear for it and I took a few guitar lessons, but I don't know what happened, I just never kept it up really. The same with the piano, I kind of have an ear for it and I might bang out a tune after trying to get it together for a couple of hours. I think each of us has a good ear for music and we all write songs – we're getting better and better every day. The band is a team effort – nobody is boss, we all help each other out.

At the start of the band, we just went crazy writing songs. We thought that we'd just write a song and all of a sudden it would be on our album, or it was going to be a single, but we didn't realise there's so much competition out there.

For people who didn't have a clue about the business to kind of go out there and compete against the big producers would have been crazy, so we're taking the safe route with the first album; it's a lot safer to get producers who are experienced. We already know a lot more than we did at the start of the band and hopefully on the second album we'll have a few of our own songs on it.

The Future

It never, ever annoys me when someone comes up to ask me for my autograph and I don't think it ever will, because when I was younger I used to absolutely yearn for it. I used to really want to be in the position that I'm in now and when people ask me for an autograph, I mean, I'm living a dream. Obviously, there are times when I'm so tired that I can't keep my eyes open, for whatever reason, and someone might come up and ask for an autograph – even at those times I feel so privileged to be in this position.

I am prepared for fame in a way, but it scares me that we've only been together a year and already my lifestyle has changed so much. I still get starstruck. I see a lot more stars now because I'm in the same industry and some people more than others make a big impression. I remember meeting Will Smith and I was astonished that I was so starstruck. I really, really like Sligo. I've seen a lot of places around the world and Sligo is still my favourite place of them all. I suppose it's because it's my home but I really love the place and the people; they're just bang on. Any time at home for me is always very enjoyable.

You get used to being away from home very quickly, obviously not straightaway, but I'm sure I'll be even more used to it in a year's time than I am now and I'm definitely a lot more used to it now than I was a year ago. I'm still getting used to this lifestyle but the main thing I want for myself, the rest of the band and my family is happiness.

Nicky Byrne

Family

I grew up in Baldoyle, which is by the seaside in north Dublin. I've got an older sister, Gillian, who's 23 and works for the airline Ryanair, and a younger brother, Adam – he's nine years old and still in school. Then, of course, there's my mam, Yvonne, who's from Coolock in Dublin, and my dad, Nicky, who's from Cabra in Dublin.

My dad is a painter and decorator. All his life he's been in a cabaret band called Nicky and Studz and he had a residency in the Racecourse Inn in Baldoyle. He used to do weddings, parties, 21sts, and I was always watching him. My mam is a housewife.

Gillian often used to sing karaoke; she has a good voice. My mam would sing at the odd wedding or so now and again. My little brother has really surprised me, he's singing away. He's a better singer than I ever was growing up and he's really into it now. He either wants to be in a band or to be an actor, or something like that.

When I was growing up, with my dad being in Nicky and Studz, I would go and help him set up the gear and set up the mic stands during the day.

Football and Leeds United

I spent most of my childhood playing sport. From the age of six I played for Home Farm in Dublin. I played right up from under-8, 9, 10, 11 and so on. I played for Home Farm for nine years. I was always a goalkeeper. Then in my final year I went to St Kelvin's, also in Dublin, and then of course Leeds United. All the Irish boys that you see at Leeds now, the likes of Stephen McPhail and Alan Maybury, I grew up with them. Then, when I went over to Leeds, Alan Smith, Harry Kewel, they were all in my digs together.

My biggest thrill was getting to Wembley in 1997 to play in the FA Cup youth final. I was always known as 'a great little goalkeeper' and that term sort of stuck. I played for Ireland Under-15s, Under-16s and Under-18s. I was very proud to represent my country. I remember playing against Portugal in Oporto and I was there listening to our national anthem facing the flag and it was just one of the proudest moments of my life.

I broke my elbow training with Ireland Under-16s, just before I went to Leeds. I was out for three months. I had an operation and I had to have two pins in my arm, although they don't set off the metal detectors at the airport for some reason! I still have a big scar there. I also broke my fingers, sprained my ankle, twisted my knee – you always got a few knocks being a goalkeeper.

I had supported Manchester United as a boy but I ended up signing a two-year professional contract with Leeds when Howard Wilkinson was manager. At the start of it I didn't mind as it was the chance of a lifetime, but I only realised how much the Leeds fans actually hated Man United when I went over there. I remember doing an interview in one of the match day programmes and I was always a big fan of Lee Sharpe. He would celebrate goals by dancing around the corner flags and all that and when I said in the programme that my favourite player was Lee Sharpe, all the Leeds fans knew I was a Man U fan. They gave me a bit of stick, but nothing too serious.

Then I became good friends with Lee Sharpe, when he signed for Leeds. I was his boot boy. I was also Gary Kelly's boot boy. It's amazing; I got on great with Sharpie. He came over to Dublin when I left Leeds. He called me and we went out. I've been out with him several times since, in Dublin and Manchester.

Gary was also great. He looked after the Irish so much. When you first go over there, you're on YT [Youth Training] wages, which isn't an awful lot of money, until you sign – which I did later – when you earn big money. But when we first went over there, Gary used to look after us; he'd buy us boots every couple of weeks, tracksuits. All the free stuff he got he'd give to us. He would come into us every day and say 'Are you homesick?', 'How are you keeping?', 'Are you missing your mam, are you missing your dad?'. He used to take us out to dinner and let us stay in his house. He was only three or four years older than us, but he was so tuned in. He had gone through everything we'd gone through, because he was actually very homesick when he first went over. I've so much time for Gary Kelly; he's such a nice guy.

But then George Graham came in as manager. My manager really was Paul Harte, the youth development officer, and Paul and I didn't really see eye to eye. Paul Harte was 6ft 5ins and I was 5ft 10ins. He always said to me, 'You need to be hitting 5ft 11ins, 6ft, all the boys in the Premiership are tall.' Schmeichel is 6ft 4ins for instance, so it was going to be difficult for me. Then, when Graham came in, he brought in his own staff and he was used to having big keepers – Nigel Martyn, John Lukic at Arsenal. David Seaman was 6ft 3ins, so I didn't fit in. My contract was up in June and I went on loan to Scarborough and

Cambridge and I didn't want to do it anymore. Football had been my life and in the previous six months singing had sort of taken over. I was writing songs in Leeds when I had some spare time. I was kind of bored there. I was living away from home, I was homesick and of course my girlfriend and my family were at home. Some nights I would cry and I was like, 'I want to go home', so eventually I did and I went back to do my Leaving Cert.

I always wanted to be a copper, to go into the Guards, but then karaoke and the band came up. When I was playing football with Leeds United, my dad was in his band, and all the boys were saying 'You should be in Boyzone, you shouldn't be a footballer'. So I ended up buying a karaoke machine and I set up a karaoke called Father and Son and my dad and I used to go around and do it. Then the auditions came up and I had the confidence by that time to go on and do it.

School

In primary school I went to Baldoyle Boys National School. The day before I started school I was knocked down, outside my house, by a guy on a pushbike, and I was in hospital for a day. So I missed the first three to four days of school. I remember the very first day

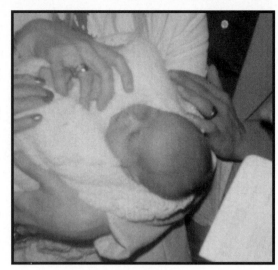

I went in and the other boys had all sort of settled and I sat beside a guy who lived on my road who I knew. I remember crying and I didn't want my mam to go and the usual kind of stuff. But I had a great primary school. I got on well with all the teachers, especially sportswise; I was always very good at football, so I used to play for the school.

I had a different teacher every year. My brother is in that school now. Last time I was home I popped back down. His teacher was my sixth class teacher, Mr O'Shea. The likes of Mr O'Donoghue, Mr Leavy, all those teachers, they were great *craic.*

Then in secondary school I went to Pobalscoil Neasáin or St Neasáin's. I was really close to my music teacher, Miss Murphy, and I still to this day haven't gone back to see her. I had Mr Kane as my year head, and he was also my football manager, so I had a great relationship with him and the principal, Mr Murphy.

Because I was playing as goalkeeper in soccer, I was also good at playing Gaelic football for the school, as I was good at catching footballs. I remember one time playing for the school against Tallaght in the semi-final of the cup and we got a penalty. Mr Murphy told me to take it and it hit the crossbar and I missed it. He never forgave me for missing that penalty!

Any time I got into trouble with the teachers I had to see my year head, Mr Kane. If I was ever sent to see him he would always say, 'You can't do that.' It was never like a pupil/teacher basis, it was more friendly; I could have a chat with him.

I never passed a music class until my Junior Cert. The thing about it was that I had to sing for the Junior Cert, because I was doing honours. That's the only reason I passed it, because I got full marks or thereabouts for singing and made it up on the paper.

I never learned any instruments, and I regret that now because I'm trying to learn how to play the piano. Kian is teaching me, he's quite good at the piano, but it's difficult for me. I never really had any great interest in the actual music side of it at school, though I was always interested in the singing side of it. I used to be in the school choir and things like that. I would look at someone playing the piano and think, 'God, how talented,' but I never had the time to do that and I just wish I was able to play it now.

I wouldn't say I was a minor celeb in school but a lot of people knew that I played for Home Farm and Ireland and it would be in the paper, like going on trial for Leeds United. I also went on trial for Derby County and I was supposed to go to Coventry, Everton and Newcastle.

They respected that I was good at football, but it never made me any different to anybody else. I certainly didn't feel different, it was just something I did. I also went to Baldoyle Secondary School. I found English quite interesting. I used to just waffle the questions, because they were so long. I was never good at maths; it just wasn't my thing. I also used to like woodwork.

I never got into trouble when I was in school, really; my mam and dad brought me up that way. I have so much respect for them, they gave me everything I ever wanted. I wasn't spoiled. I wasn't from a rich family nor from a poor family, I was from an everyday family. But my mam always brought me up to believe: 'You're not better than anybody else and nobody's better than you – they might have more money or a nicer car, or they might be better off, but as a person they're not better than you.'

That always stuck with me. I have so much respect for my mam. I never once went on the hop from school. It just wasn't me. I never went 'knacker drinking', I just couldn't. My mam always said, 'If you ever want a drink, you can have it in the house.' That was when I was about 15 or 16.

In school I was a bit of a messer. I was always with a group of lads and I would be the one to make the jokes in class and everybody would laugh and the teacher used to not have a go at me. They didn't hate me. I always got on with every teacher, but if ever I got into trouble I'd give a little smile and say 'Sorry' and they used to let me get away with it.

My best friends from school are still my best friends today: Colm 'Cos' Costello from Donaghmede, who lives near to where Keith Duffy and Shane Lynch are from, and Sean O'Grady. His nickname is 'Skinner' and he lives around the corner from me.

I had left after fifth year to go to Leeds, so when I came back I went to St Plunkett's College in Whitehall for a year. I went there to do my Leaving Cert, even though it was a repeat class. That was hard for me as well, because I had been a professional footballer for two years and I had been earning great money.

Then, to get up every morning, get the train from Killester from Bayside and the bus to Whitehall and then walk down to St Plunkett's, it was hard, but I did it for a year. I got a great Leaving Cert and I did the Garda exam, passed that and actually last March, just before 'Swear It Again' was released, my mam got a thing in the post to say that I had to start in Templemore [police training college]. It was amazing to see.

Ronan only told me a while ago that he too wanted to be a Guard, and I was going 'No way!' because that's everything I've ever wanted to do. A lot of people say I look a bit like Ronan so that was weird, it frightens me!

FROM TOP TO BOTTOM: Nicky and Alan Maybury playing for Ireland; Nicky's debs (high school ball), 1997, wearing a suit like that of Richard Gere in the film *An Officer and a Gentleman*; at home with Mam, Dad, Nana, Gillian and Adam

RIGHT: Youth FA Cup winners, 1997. Nicky placed in front row, first from left

OPPOSITE PAGE: Nicky with Taoiseach (Irish Prime Minister) Bertie Ahern

Work

I never even had a paper round. My first job was as a professional footballer. I went when I was 16 and a half. I signed pro when I was 17 and spent two years at it. I did actually work in a shop in Dublin for two months, called Alias Tom Menswear. I was working there in the summer. I came home in the June, so I was working July and August and then I went back to school in September.

How We Met

I was still in school when Boyzone came out. I remember when Boyzone were first on the *Late Late Show* (November 1993) and my mam taped it for my sister, and I used to rewind it over and over again. I am about two or three years younger than Ronan, and five years younger than Keith Duffy. Boyzone started when I was about 13, I think Ronan was 16 and he was the youngest. But watching them, I always wanted to be in the band. I used to say to my mates, being the hard chaw, 'Look at the state of them,' and all my mates were laughing, saying 'Yeah, yeah.' But I was secretly thinking, 'This is brilliant, this is what I want to do.'

For about the first year of Boyzone, I never admitted to liking them though I never said I didn't like them, but I was such a fan. Then it grew from there. When I went to Leeds, I had all their albums, all the singles; I used to sing them constantly. All the other boys liked dance music and I was playing the Boyzone ballads.

The first time I met Ronan was in Tamango's nightclub in Dublin. It was soon after his mam died and he had just married Yvonne. I was about to start my Leaving Cert. I had seen every other one of them in person before. When I worked in a shop in town, Stephen would come in to buy clothes. I had met Keith and Shane a few times in Donaghmede and I met Mikey in a nightclub years ago.

I had never met Ronan and he was the one that I had always wanted to meet, I respected him so much. Then in Tamango's – I still have to tell Ronan this! – I went up to Ronan and said, 'Can I shake your hand? I have great respect for you, you're a credit to the

country and all the best,' and I said something like, 'I'm sorry to hear about your mam, the best of luck with Yvonne.' He said, 'You're a good guy, thanks for coming over.' That was the first time I met Ronan.

The first record I ever bought was Kylie Minogue's 'I Should Be So Lucky'. I also had her album. I used to love Jason Donovan too. All the things that the average normal guys growing up didn't like I seemed to like. They were like, 'Jason Donovan! He's . . .' whatever. I loved Bros too. My sister was a huge fan of Bros, although I was bit too young. All I remember is the torn jeans and the songs. I loved Aha as well. I used to get a spare tape and sit in my room and put on the radio at ten o'clock at night and tape all the slow songs. I wasn't really into dance music, although I am now and I have a lot of favourite tunes – back then it was just slow songs. I used to be in my room, pretending I was on stage, pretending I was in East 17, which is funny to think of now.

Looking back, I don't know how I ever did it; I think, 'Jesus, how lucky I was'. I was doing karaoke and I was singing constantly and gaining so much confidence. My dad and myself were doing local schools, 21sts and socials. There was a thing about the audition for the

band on the radio and I rang the guy and asked what I had to do. He said, 'Right, what you have to do is do a demo tape, record two or three songs and send in a picture of yourself.'

I had all the karaoke equipment, so I set it up in my house one day and I sang for about ten or 12 hours, working on the songs. I sang 'Isn't It a Wonder?' by Boyzone, and I sang two Irish songs acappella – 'The Town I Loved So Well' and 'She Moved Through the Fair'.

I sent the tape off and then they rang me and said, 'come to the audition.' I went along to the audition for a new traditional band they wanted to form, which was called Ceol. It wasn't for the new boy band, IOU. Louis was there and I sang 'Father and Son' by Boyzone and then I sang 'She Moved Through the Fair'. Then Louis called me down and said he was setting up a new boy band called IOU and they were looking for one more person and would I like to meet them. I said, 'Of course.'

It's funny, because when Louis called me over and introduced himself and all the rest and I went 'Louis Walsh!' I couldn't believe it. Then he said to me, 'I'm setting up this new pop band,' but I thought he said 'pub band'! There was a photographer there from the *Evening Herald*. Louis turned to him and said I was going to be in this new band, what I thought he'd said was a 'pub band,' and to get a picture. I was standing there and everyone was looking at me and I thought, 'I don't want to be in a pub band!'

Then I went for the second audition, which was for IOU, and Bryan and me were the first two to sing and they couldn't choose between us. It was in the papers: 'BATTLE OF THE BLONDS'. Bryan and myself were actually good friends, because I knew him from karaoke. We weren't the best of friends, but I did know him fairly well. It was mad, because Louis wanted me or Bryan and some of the guys wanted Bryan, some of the guys wanted me. They couldn't choose.

So we went down to Sligo to live with them for a while, two or three weeks. Then the guys came up to Dublin and they wanted the two of us, a harmony vocal they thought. Everybody could sing, the harmonies were brilliant and they got rid of one of the other guys from Sligo.

The type of person I am, I can get on with anybody from the start, I'm an easy-going person but I did wonder what the Sligo guys would think, whether they'd want two Dubliners in the band, and me and Bryan felt the same. But singing together, we couldn't believe the music we were making. The sound was amazing and Louis thought it was fantastic. We then started showcasing for record companies.

When the band first started out,

we were rehearsing every day in the Red Box and Shane and Mark used to live in my house. Kian lived with Bryan and then went to live in his auntie's house in Blackrock.

So we just had this bond all the time together. My mam and dad went to Tenerife on holiday, about a month into the band, so I had my dad's car and I was insured on it. I used to go around picking all the guys up, from my house to Bryan's house, to Mark's house, out to the Pod and then drop them back.

It was just brilliant, to look back at it then. We owe everything to our parents, because they funded us through the whole thing. We didn't earn a penny until we signed the record deal in October 1998. When I was in Leeds I was a big fan of designer clothes and I remember saying to all the boys that I was wearing Dolce e Gabbana or whatever because of the Leeds days. They were like, 'What a waste of money, paying £100 or whatever on a pair of trousers,' but now they're just as bad!

I was very lucky out of all the boys, because when I was with Home Farm, we were always in Liverpool and Blackpool, I played for Ireland in Portugal, Belgium, Switzerland, Sweden, Denmark, so I had been to those places for a couple of days. Most of the boys in the band had not been outside Ireland or the UK. I also went to Spain a few times with my family and I had been to Canada. Now, taking off with the band, we're all over the place. So I've seen a lot at a very young age, and again the five of us are very, very lucky to be in the position we're in today.

The Future

A lot of people change around you when you get into bands like this, but my friends are just normal. When I get home I go to the pub or for a game of snooker with Cos and Skinner. They ask about the band but they're not gobsmacked by it like other people. They don't want to know 'What's it like doing this?' or 'What's it like meeting this person?'. I've been driving since I passed my test at the age of 17. When I signed the record deal, I bought a Peugeot 306 convertible sports car. I had it for about two or three months. Ronan helped me out on it – he managed to get me a good deal. Then I thought, 'I'm never home.' 'Swear It Again' was just about to happen and I sold the car. I will get another, but I'll wait until things get less busy.

The last year has been beyond my wildest dreams. It has been a roller-coaster ride. It's been the best year I could ever think of. It's very hard work, though, you get up early in the morning, back into bed late and things like that are tough.

But it's amazing. I couldn't ask for any more. I'm the luckiest person alive. I thank my mam and dad, and my brother and sister, for the person I am today. It's just amazing and it seems to be getting bigger and bigger. We've had three number ones in Ireland and Britain. It's blown us away and hopefully it can continue and we can become as big as Boyzone, and if we do become as big as Boyzone then we want to be bigger. We want to be the biggest band in the world. We don't know if we can do it, but we can definitely try.

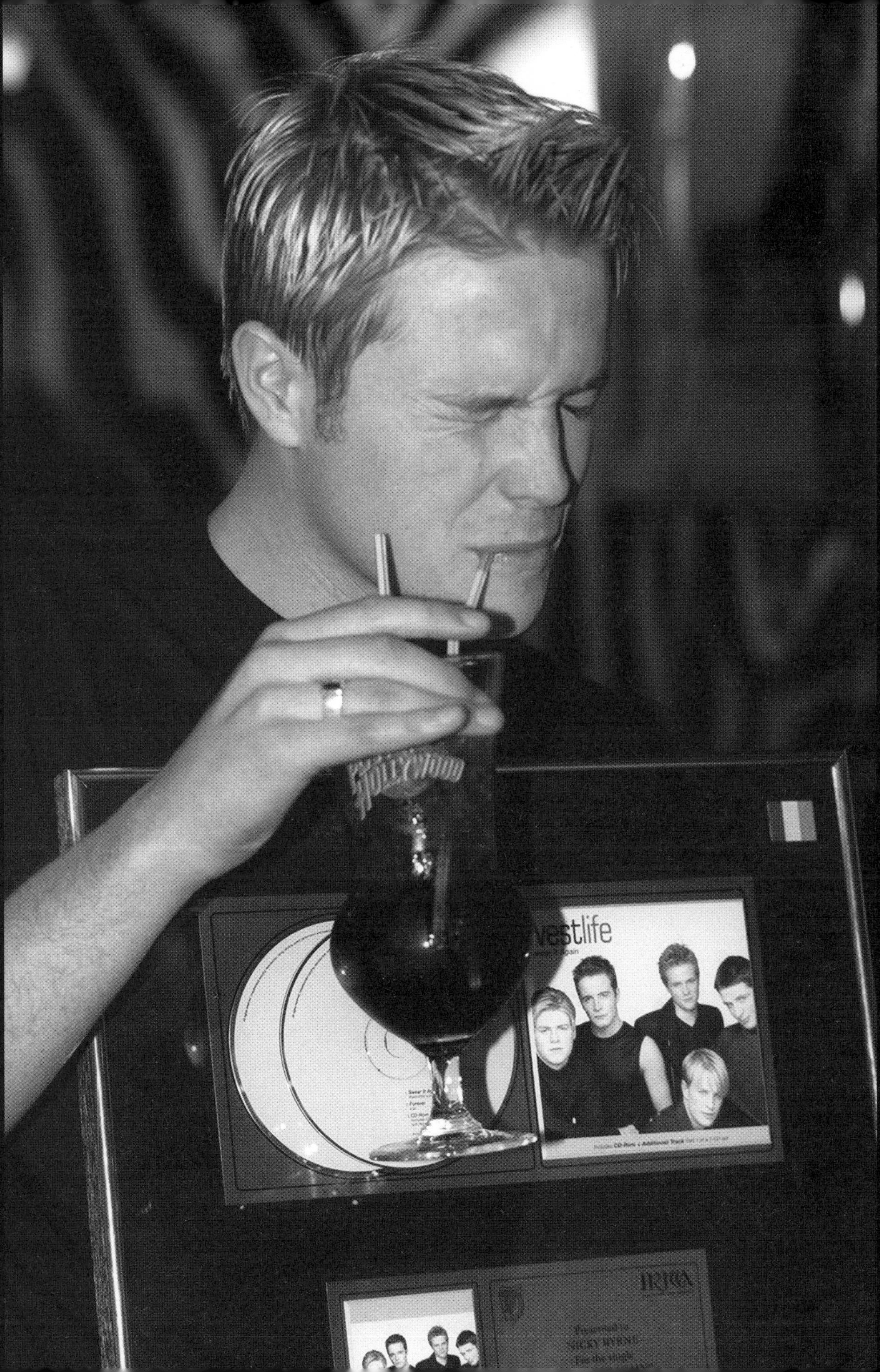
westlife
Presented to
NICKY BYRNE
For the single

Bryan McFadden

Family

I'm from Artane in north Dublin. I've just one sister. Her name is Susan. She is aged 16 and she is in her last year in school.

Susan and I have always been into dancing and we both joined the Billie Barry school of dancing when we were quite young in Dublin. Susan played Annie in the musical at the Olympia and later she got the lead part in their pantomime for a couple of years. She's absolutely delighted about me being in Westlife, but compared to me she's very, very quiet.

My mum's name is Mairead and she is from Co. Tipperary. She works as a playschool teacher. My dad's name is Brendan and he's what you would call the territory manager for a major pharmaceutical company.

Artane is a pretty rough area and I had few friends there. It was okay growing up. I used to be a real trickster when I was younger and I was always up to devilment, like putting stones in pints of milk on doorsteps.

My best friend growing up — and he's still my best friend to this day — lived up the road from me. His name is Eddie Loughlan and we've been mates since we were aged about three. We do everything together — we're kind of soul mates.

School — and My Weight Problem

The first school I went to was called St Fiachra's. I can remember well my first day at school there as I got thrown out of my class for throwing an elastic band at the teacher. I think her name was Miss Barry. Then I went to St David's CBS primary school. English was my best subject there, but I hated Irish. I then went across the road to St David's secondary school for a year. But I hated the place and the teachers. The Christian Brothers didn't treat me very well.

When I was growing up I got a lot of hassle because I was overweight. The abuse I got for being fat was unbelievable. That's why I was always cheeky as a kid – giving smart answers back – and that's why I always got into trouble. There was many a time I got bullied, until I got to fifth or sixth class when I became taller and filled out.

I know what overweight people feel like. I see a lot of them and I know they will come out better people because of their experience. I got more confident from being put down time and time again, after getting so much abuse and slagging. But it all just bounced off me. It didn't bother me that much when people slagged me – they never really had a nickname for me, it was the usual taunts such as 'Fatso!' I think young people in school who are getting the same type of abuse should take no notice of it. Look at how I've turned out!

I went to St Joseph's Rosmini for the remaining four years I was in secondary school. Rosmini deals with a lot of visually impaired children mixed into the classes. There were three or four visually impaired kids in my class. Some of the kids were more impaired than others; some were even blind. I became quite good friends with some of them, and a whole group of us used to go into town drinking. One of the visually impaired lads was an excellent footballer. I had one really good visually impaired friend there, Stephen, who I still meet now and again.

I was all right at school but to be honest my mind always seemed to be elsewhere. When I was doing my Leaving Cert, it was the week of the auditions for the band. I remember my last exam was construction studies and I ended up cramming about the whole lot into an hour and a half, when it should have taken three hours, as the next day it was being decided what the line-up for the band was.

Sport

I played loads of sport when I was younger. Once, when I was in secondary school, I was on nine different teams. I played badminton, I was on two of the three Gaelic football teams, I played soccer, I was on the swimming team and I was also on the table tennis team.

I was the kind of guy who was never the best at any type of sport – if I was on a football team I'd be an average player. From fourth class I did swimming. I was always a fast swimmer, maybe because I had big arms and it was around that time that I started to lose weight and become leaner, so I wasn't embarrassed about showing off my body.

I was quite good at table tennis. There was a German guy on the Rosmini team who was ranked number one on the German team and I was number two to him on our school team. There were four of us on that team and we won the Dublin championships.

Work

My first real job was when I was aged about 17, in a cash and carry store in Phibsboro. One interesting job I used to have was helping out at bingo in Whitehall. It was a pretty nice earner too – £15 an hour. I'm pretty used to the bingo lingo by now! Every night there were seven girls on and one guy – so I had a good laugh chatting up the girls.

I probably knew most of the grannies too! Every Thursday my mam went to Whitehall bingo and I'd always wanted to go and see the place because it looked massive from the outside, so it was really weird that I ended up working there. Then during, and just after, my Leaving Cert I started working as a security guard with McDonald's. I was working from six o'clock in the evening until four o'clock in the morning.

My folks were very wary about me working there. They had every right to be as a few times I nearly got killed. I got bottles on the head and stuff. I worked in outlets in O'Connell Street, Grafton Street and the ILAC Centre. I used to work in the ILAC Centre during the day on my own and it got robbed a few times. They would run in and rob the till. I actually ran out after them one day, and there was a guy working in the shop opposite, he ran with me and the two of us ran into a flat complex after the robbers. But the place was so rough looking that we shot back out like a bullet.

The incident where I was nearly killed happened late one night when there were actually two of us on, in Grafton Street. Five guys from the north came along and we wouldn't let them in because they were all drunk. I said, 'No, you're not coming in.' So they started to force open the door and a couple of them tried to put their feet in. So I grabbed one of them by the neck and with that another guy came along, smashed a bottle and threw it at me. It hit the wall. I had a very lucky escape.

I hated fighting. A friend had recommended me for the job. You have to remember that I'm 6' 2" now and that helps with that kind of job. My friend knew I needed the money at the time because I was only starting off in the band. As well as that I needed a job where I could work late at night, an after-hours job, so I could have the day free for the band. But I didn't realise I was going to be working Saturday nights. Even at school I never got into any fights, I absolutely hated it. I never started on anyone. I can defend myself, I can definitely handle myself, but I don't like fighting.

How We Met

My mam put me into the Billie Barry school of dancing when I was aged about six and then Susan joined later. There were a lot of boys in it. There were 10 boys in my class and 30 girls. I was in it for years and we used to do loads of pantomimes and usually appeared on the *Late Late Show*.

A lot of people who've now become famous went to the Billie Barry

school in the recent past – Keavy and Edele from B*Witched, Keri Ann, Angeline Ball and, of course, Mikey Graham from Boyzone. Mikey was a few years ahead of me and it's pretty weird that I've ended up in a boy band just like he has.

I was always into music as a kid and around 1997 I formed a band called Cartel. Two other guys formed it with me – Dara Dean and Tim Madigan. We were a bit like the Backstreet Boys and we used to play all over Dublin. We built up a big fan base in Ireland. We used to dance in a place called Dance Nation in Parnell Square. Some of the guys from OTT and Dove also used to dance there. Jim Hutton was the man in charge of the place and from doing karaoke there – I used to do a Gary Barlow song – it was he who suggested that the three of us form a band. He said he knew Louis Walsh and that he could get us introduced.

The funny thing is I actually went to see Backstreet Boys playing in Dublin and I saw IOU supporting them. I remember laughing at the guys when they came on stage. It wasn't that they were bad or good, but there were six of them on stage and a boy band with six didn't make any sense. To be honest with you I didn't even listen to them. I watched them for a couple of minutes, saw there were six of them and said, 'I'm out of here!' and I went to the toilet. When I came back they were finished.

A lot of people did turn their noses up at boy bands and didn't have a lot of time for them. I never went to see Take That, even though I wanted to go. I don't think I had the bottle to go as it was 100 per cent girls going to Take That. But I did go to Boyzone's first concert in The Point with a friend. The boys gave Susan tickets when she was doing Annie in the Olympia – they'd come in and met her backstage. She couldn't go because she was on the stage, so a friend and I went.

The security guards on the door asked us if we were gay. They were being serious as well. I just kept my head down; I had a hat on. They were taking the piss out of us for going to see Boyzone. It didn't upset me, back then I suppose it was understandable – Boyzone were fellows for girls.

Around that time I was starring in a TV programme on RTE called *Finbar's Class*. That lasted a year and I played a character called Spot. I had also been going out to Gibney's pub in Malahide and it was there that I met Nicky and his dad doing karaoke. I used to sit down the back but then I started doing warm-up sessions with Nicky or his dad. It was great fun.

TOP: Bryan, aged six, on a Donegal beach with Susan
BOTTOM: Bryan at the age of three with his young friend Alan Dodd
INSET: Bryan, aged three, having a good time at a funfair in Hastings in England

I saw things in the paper about this new band being formed by Louis Walsh and that there was a lot of interest. I had already sent Louis photographs and tapes of our band, Cartel. Originally I wanted to get him to manage Cartel but he wasn't up for a new band. So he said, 'If you want to come and try an audition, come along.' It was still IOU at the time when I heard about the auditions.

I was totally up for it. I knew there was a record deal on the cards.

When you've just finished school and you want something new, it's exciting. At the auditions I sang 'Father and Son' and 'Words'. They got everyone to do those two songs. If I'd had a choice, I probably would have done a Backstreet Boys song or a Gary Barlow song.

The weird thing is that Nicky and I ended up at the auditions. Neither of us knew the other was going. There were two auditions and at the first one I saw Nicky at it and I said to him, 'What are you doing here?' He said, 'I'm going for the audition.' I said, 'So am I, you never told me!'

I thought Nicky was going to get it before me, because the place was just for one person at first. But I was thinking to myself, 'It would be great if the two of us got it.' We never thought that was going to happen. Originally, the band was supposed to be going to England to do a concert for *Smash Hits* and we're going, 'It would be great to be getting up on stage with them.' Nicky was a Boyzone fan. I think the lads saw that I was a Backstreet Boys fan and they liked that. They were basically looking for my funkiness.

Louis and Kian liked Nicky and the rest of the

57

guys wanted me. One of the things at the audition was singing and dancing. The two of us sang, that was grand, and the two of us danced but Nicky hadn't a clue.

That was the second day of the auditions. They had just picked the two of us and told the rest of them to go. It went very, very fast. It was very weird that Nicky and I were left to the last two. Our friendship, it didn't go away, but there was no communication between the two of us. It was kind of like 'How can I say anything – one of us is going to go.'

But then we went to Sligo with the lads, and we kind of knew the way it was going. There were four of the Sligo guys and so, including Nicky and myself, there were six in the band.

We knew that the two of us were fitting in a lot better with Shane, Kian and Mark. Then the six of us were sat down and Louis said, 'Right, I'm picking my band now.' He said, 'To start with, Shane, Kian, Mark and Bryan are in the band.' Then he said that Nicky was being picked above Michael. But everyone knew that Nicky was better by far. The only reason I was picked was because I was the dancer and because I was into low harmonies and fitted in.

It was a sad day for Michael. I actually got on very, very well with Michael. I went out with him when I was down in Sligo and everything. We became good friends. I felt really, really bad, but at the end of the day, inside, I knew that this was a make or break opportunity, an absolute golden opportunity.

We had already been told that we'd be supporting Boyzone and at that stage I was thinking, 'I'm going to be on this huge stage supporting Boyzone and we're going to be playing to these huge crowds.'

I thought we'd get to number 38 or 39, that we'd get into the Top 40 and maybe go on *Top of the Pops*. Then as things went on we did the *Smash Hits* tour and we found out we were in for the Best Newcomer award, which we eventually won. It was like, 'Oh, my God!' Then people started saying we'd get into the Top Ten.

I remember our first time on *Top of the Pops*, when 'Swear It Again' went straight in at number one. It was always my dream to appear on *Top of the Pops*, and here we were not only appearing on it but at number one as well. Everyone was really friendly to us on the show, particularly the band Faithless.

The Future

I have never changed. A lot of people call me the joker in the band and I think that's because I was always the smart alec growing up. I got so much stick and slagging in school because I was fat when I was young that I always had to have a smart answer to hit back at the other person. I'm now really good at one liners. That's my way. Because I was so used to getting abuse, and instead of taking it and feeling bad, I'd throw it back at them and make them feel as bad as I did. It just came naturally after a while. Fame hasn't gone to my head so far, from the day we thought 'This is great' on the *Smash Hits* tour, supporting Boyzone.

The main thing I want to do when this is all over is look after my family. Susan will naturally want to work but I never want to see her go without anything she wants. The same goes for my parents. My dad has worked hard all his life, trying to keep us happy and put food on the table.

I don't come from a very rich family; I come from an ordinary family in Dublin. When we were growing up we had a holiday every year, but it was mainly down the country in Ireland. We occasionally went to Spain or Portugal, but that was only a few times. Now I want them to have the best of everything. I want to see my family being happy and for me to look after them as much as possible.

I've four great friends now in Westlife and I'm enjoying every minute of it.

Girls! Girls! Girls!

Kian

My first kiss happened when I was aged nine at the back of the Mervin community centre in Sligo. No names will be mentioned, not on the first kiss! The first long-term relationship I had was with a girl called Sonia, from Carton in Sligo. I went out with her for over a year. I was about 15. It was quite a serious relationship, but we were very mature about it. We used to see each other every night; we would take a cycle to the beach during the summer or go to the cinema. I used to collect her from school and walk her home. We'd do our homework and then we'd meet up.

It was what I would call love. I think as far as I am concerned I was in love with her and she broke up with me when I was about 16 and a half and it broke my heart. It took me a long time to get over her. We broke up because she felt we were too young to be going out with each other for such a long time. Just 16 years of age and going out with each other for a year and a half. She felt that way but I didn't and I kept on trying to get her back but it didn't work.

About eight months later I started going out with another girl, Yvonne, for about a year. The same thing happened. I broke off with her three times and she broke off with me in the end and I was devastated. Then the band started and I kind of got away from it all.

There were two serious relationships – I also went out with a girl in Dublin, who I quite liked, for about three months. It was around the time of our first Boyzone tour, and I was gone for three weeks. She didn't like it. Then there was this thing that I couldn't walk down the street holding hands with her and she didn't like that either. I haven't had a serious relationship since.

I would like to be in a relationship, because it gets very lonely on the road. To be able to pick up the phone and ring someone that's not family or friends – your girlfriend – is a great thing, and Nicky's very lucky to have that. He's got a lot of companionship there. To go home and have a girl that you can trust, who isn't going to go selling their story to the paper the next day.

This has already happened to me, in Bristol. A girl sold her story to the *News of the World*. The thing was that at that stage we were fresh in the business. We didn't know what it was like and we didn't know that we were actually going to do what we've done. I am wary now about one-night stands; that's one thing about having a girlfriend, it's not a one-night stand, it's someone you can trust, someone you've got companionship with. There's a cuddle involved: 'It's not for what I do, it's for who I am.'

I was annoyed about the girl in the *News of the World*. She said something about 007, that she did this James Bond move on me and that she squeezed my naked ribcage with her hips! I was reading it and I was going, 'This girl is going into detail here and she doesn't care.' Most of it was total crap. I laughed it off; at least she said I was good – she said I went five times, like! I was very, very annoyed for a few days and I wanted to get away and a lot of people were reading the article and going, 'Oh, look at you. Is it true? Is it true?' But I mean, we were big enough to make the front page of the *News of the World*; that's one way I looked at it.

Shane rang me at 11 o'clock and said, 'Just go down and get the *News of the World* and ring me back.' I was expecting some other story. My mam was quite annoyed at first, she looked at it, looked at me and saw the annoyance in me and how I was hurt inside, and she said, 'It will be okay, don't worry about it.' My dad looked at it and said, 'It's only a load of rubbish, son, don't heed it. At least you're big enough to make the front page of the *News of the World*. Don't heed it,' and he threw it away.

But I was so annoyed that day and everybody was kind of looking at me and showing me the paper and asking if it was true and sticking it up against their windows as I was passing their houses. Luckily, we were going to England the next day and the paper there hadn't printed it.

When I was younger I lost my virginity with someone I loved. I'm glad I did, I don't regret it at all. That was a personal thing. When it came to things like that and you were talking with your mates, they'd be going, 'Oh, what did you do, what happened, what happened?' and you'd say, 'Oh, nothing, lads!' You wouldn't exactly tell. I was in a serious relationship at the time. I was aged 16 and that was personal business between my girlfriend and me.

I would like to get married and settle down one day. At the moment my career is too important to me. I've got to go with this band. I could give someone commitment for four or five years and not have kids and not get married, that wouldn't be a problem to me. But the thing about it is I would never ask a girl to go through what I do, because it's so much pressure.

I think for me to have a proper relationship with someone outside the business would be very, very hard. But for me to have a relationship with somebody inside the business, whether it's in music or acting or whatever, it's in our line and circle of work. They would understand a lot more. They wouldn't be like, 'Were you with this girl in Germany?' or get upset when people are saying they've done this and that with me when it's not true.

I have enormous sympathy for what happened to Stephen Gateley. He was very brave in what he did. He's a good friend of the band's. We're 100 per cent behind him and no matter what he does in his personal life, that's his personal life and that's the way we look at it.

Nicky

I first met Georgina Ahern when we were in Scoil Neasáin in north Dublin. I met her when I was in first year. The thing about it was that I always liked her, but I never spoke to her until third year. I used to see her in the corridor every day and we would say hello to each other or nod or whatever, but I remember I got one of my mates, Cos, to ask her out for me and she said no. That was grand, so I left it for a year and then she said yeah, eventually. So the first time I went out with her was the day before my 16th birthday. It was 8 October, I was 16 on the ninth. One of my friends was having a house party and everybody from school was invited to the house and I had arranged to meet her that day, so it was great.

It's funny being the only one in the band in a stable relationship, because the rest of the lads look at me and they envy me in a way, because when you're on the road, it does get very, very hard. You need somebody to talk to, to chill out with at night, to wind down.

Georgina's always there for me. She was there for me when I came home from Leeds. I was devastated, I was down, I was crying. I didn't know where I was going with my life. She was always there for me. So the boys all look at that; when we're on tour or anything, I can ring Georgina at any time, at night time, and have a good old chat.

Then there's the other part and the boys are meeting new girls. I'm a very friendly guy and I'll chat to anybody all night, but I know I'll never be

with them or anything. So it's good for me. I'm happy in the position I'm in.

We don't see each other a lot, that's the only thing. It does get hard. We were on the Boyzone tour, then we went to Asia for a month, so we were away for two and a half months, and she was in America for two and a half months, so we were on opposite sides of the world. I was in Japan, she was in Boston. I was in Australia and she was in Boston, and you're totally dependent on telephones.

As for the fans, so far so good. The fans are great to me. I have a great fan base, bigger than I ever expected to have, having a girlfriend. They're very nice to Georgina, no one has ever said anything bad. They bought her presents at Christmas time. Fans always buy your mam and dad presents and bottles of wine and things for Christmas and they did that with Georgina as well last Christmas.

They seemed to have accepted her because we like to describe ourselves as a modern-day boy band. We're not about taking our tops off and dancing around the stage, like boy bands were in the past. Time moves on. If we were to do that now it wouldn't work. We're more about the music and our harmonies, and people respect our music and if you have a girlfriend you have a girlfriend. Why lie to people? You want to be honest with them.

When I first went to Leeds I'd been going out with Georgina for about nine months and I flew home and never told her – I went to her house to surprise her. When I called to her house she was in the shower, so I went up to her room and just sat on the bed. A few minutes later she came in and she was totally shocked, because I hadn't seen her in a month.

I always seem to be away for Valentine's Day and for her birthday. I fill her bedroom with balloons. We like to go out to dinner. We like to spend good quality time together, go out at

weekends if we get a chance. It's a good relationship. You do naturally feel a bit more in the spotlight because Georgina is the daughter of Bertie Ahern [Taoiseach/Prime Minister of Ireland]. I wasn't too apprehensive about that when I joined the band because it was in the papers at the start when I was a footballer that I was going out with Bertie's daughter, and then, when I came home, I was so used to going out to things with Bertie. Like out at football matches, there was always press snapping him. They never really snapped me and Georgina. Then, since the band started off, the photographers always seem to want the three of us together. The last time was in Croke Park in Dublin and the photographers seemed to be snapping me and Bertie rather than the game. I get on great with Bertie, he's a great football fan as well.

I can remember my first kiss as a kid. It was with my mam's friend's daughter, Debbie. I was about nine or ten. I had about three or four steady girlfriends when I was very young. For about a month or so, nothing serious. Georgina was my first serious girlfriend.

Like all the lads I went to the local disco when I was 13, 14, 15, 16; we all went to meet girls. I used to go to the leisure centre in Portmarnock and a place in Howth. I must have been about 15 – before I started going out with Georgina – when I went to this disco in Dublin called The Furnace, which has closed down now. It was to celebrate our exam results. It was one of those nights when everybody goes mad. I must have snogged about 11 girls. I don't think it was any more than that!

I would naturally like to get married, settle down and have kids, but not in the next three, four or five years. You never can tell, though, maybe it will happen, look at Ronan, I'm sure he didn't know he was going to get married so young. But I will eventually settle down.

Shane

I was in a serious relationship when I was about 15 or 16, for about a year and a half. Her name was Helena. I always wanted to be free and to have more than one fling. I was never into having relationships, I was into shifting one girl and moving on to the next. When I was younger I used to flick straight to the lingerie section in my mum's catalogues. I thought it was deadly. That was my first glimpse of real women! When I was about aged 14, if I was with one girl I'd always end up with three or four of her friends, one after the other. In fact, I once went out with one girl just because I fancied her best friend. It was the easiest way to get near her. Now, a lot of girls do come up to you, so you've just got to know who's who and know what's what.

I always seemed to get nice girls when I was younger. I wasn't the babe-puller in the town or anything like that, nothing like it; but I always ended up with a decent girl: 70 per cent were good-looking girls. It's deadly now, you go out and people want to talk to you and you meet a lot of gorgeous women: just kind of talk to them and you know within five minutes whether they're genuine.

I am a bit envious that Nicky is in a relationship. Nicky and Georgina have been together for five years now, which is deadly. I don't know how he does it. In a way I'd like that myself, I'd like a girlfriend, but I can see how hard it would be. I don't know if I'd be able to start a relationship now and be away from somebody for that long. Nicky's got a foundation of five years and they're getting on great.

If I get married I'd live in Ireland, hopefully, but it depends how the band goes. Sometimes I'd like to live in Ireland and other times I say if the band becomes huge, it might not be practical. I will definitely still live here in Sligo for a few years and if I get a lot of money, I'll build a house for my family in Sligo and have a house in Dublin.

You get a few mad ones among our fans; they just want to be around you and be close to you. We've had the cars following us around. On tour in Europe we had 19 cars following us! They were every nationality, Spanish, Italian, a lot of Germans. You get all that, but it's brilliant.

We've become famous very, very quickly. We went from nothing to two number one singles, everything has gone really fast and I just hope it keeps going. We go to America, Europe, we have an album, a tour, the next year is vital to us.

We're only young. If you're going to shift girls, that's the way it is. But if some girl goes to the paper and makes up some story, you can't really help it; you just have to let it go over your head. I mean, if that's what they want to do and people believe them, the paper will accept it. It does worry me: if ever I want to find a serious, long-term girlfriend, it will worry me big time because you don't know whether to trust them. It mightn't just be gold-diggers, it might just to be involved with the band, to be around and say, 'I'm with Westlife'. Some girls are like that and that's what they want, but then there's the others who are genuine and say, 'Fair enough, you're in a band, but I actually like you.'

You have to be very careful. Like, I know straightaway whether a girl is there to talk to me or to talk to one of Westlife. I can tell within five minutes; it's usually so obvious and she says the wrong things, so I just know.

I do worry about it, definitely, to find a wife in ten years' time or whatever. You could be going out with a girl and think you are in love with her and then you could say 'This is the one for me' and five or six years after you're married you realise, 'Oh, my God, I'm not in Westlife anymore' and she goes, 'Bye!' Like, that could happen.

As for famous people the band like, well Kian used to like Britney Spears when she started off and Bryan used to copy Kian. Mark loves Mariah Carey while I think Catherine Zeta Jones is a class girl.

Mark

It's really weird because I never thought that I'd be in a band where there'd be a few girls waiting outside the hotel. I never realised that I'd be in a position where somebody would want my autograph, so that's really strange and it's a big privilege. We try to give the fans as much time as they want because, obviously, if they weren't there to support us then there'd be no point in us going on because it just wouldn't be worth while. All of us love music and we'd love to be able to say we could do it without any support just as long as we're in a band, but at the end of the day you can't be a successful band unless you have support. So if fans come along to see us at a TV show, unless we're rushing off afterwards we'll always stop and have a chat and get a few pictures done and sign a few pieces of paper or whatever and go out and have a chat with them outside the hotel or wherever.

The fact that we're a new band now means that because we have such a hard and heavy schedule we don't have an awful lot of time and we're usually very tired when we get back to the hotel, but we do spend as much time as possible with them.

I do really love Mariah Carey. I love everything about her, I really love the way she performs and her expressions. I finally met her for the first time recently at the launch of the MTV Europe Music Awards in London. I fell in love with her music and I just became a big fan.

The first kiss I had was on a holiday. I was no more than 11, 12 or 13 and it was on that French exchange trip I went on at school. She was Irish too. It was really weird, not what I expected at all. It was disgusting for about two seconds, then I went, 'Wait a minute, this is lovely' and so I kept on doing it. I can't remember exactly where she was from or her name.

In Sligo, every time I came across a girl that I liked and if she liked me, of course, I'd have a snog. I never had a preference for blondes or any type particularly. I never said, 'You're not blonde so I'm not going to be with you' or 'I only like girls with brown hair so go away, even though you're good looking and you're a very nice person'. If I got on well with the girl and we had a good laugh and I liked her or whatever, then we'd have a snog. I didn't have very many long-term relationships at all. I just have the kind of motto, when you're young have a ball, because there's loads of time for settling down when you're older.

One Hallowe'en night my mates and I got talking to this group of girls and we all snogged one of them. Then we went off and we bumped into another group of girls and I snogged this girl who I later found out was the first girl's cousin. Then we went on to a nightclub and I snogged another girl — she wasn't connected, thank goodness!

Obviously, you can't help it if you fall in love with someone but I think there's loads of time for all that crap when you're older. The funny thing is I have never actually been in love with a girl. Sometimes I'd say 'Wait a minute, I really like this person' but then all of a sudden I'd realise it was just a phase or whatever.

You don't necessarily have to get married but I definitely do want to get married and settle down and have kids. I haven't actually thought about it. I suppose I don't really want to get married until I'm about 30 at least. I just want to have a great time while I'm younger, experience everything.

Bryan

When I was at school I was always called ugly because I was overweight. Believe it or not my first kiss was when I was 17. It wasn't because I was a late developer or anything, it was just that a girl wouldn't look twice at me and I didn't have the confidence.

But then, when I hit 17, I got taller and leaner and found it easier to chat up girls. Even though I was 17 when I had my first kiss I certainly made up for it. I can't tell you who she was, nor can I tell you who my first girlfriend was. I like to remain a bit secretive!

But it did hurt when I was younger. You know you think you're so ugly. I used to get called 'ugliest bloke' and I'd take it seriously and I'd be offended and feel really bad. I never went to discos when I was younger as I wasn't into that. I also wasn't really interested in any of the girls in my area. Now, it's totally turned around, and from being the ugliest bloke in the class to having thousands of girls screaming at me, it just feels great.

Smash Hits have polls and I came No. 17 in the most handsome blokes poll. I mightn't have come highest in the band, like Shane and Kian came higher than me, but to see myself at No. 17! I beat people like Brad Pitt, I know it's only a bit of fun — there was a huge chart of pictures and I was counting down from 100 and I got to No. 17 and straightaway I thought back to the days when I was called ugly.

When we started out with the band it used to be me and Kian who would go to all the nightclubs and chat up the girls, now it's Mark and me. It would just be to go and look for good-looking girls and do your best. Not to settle down, but to look for friendship and maybe a kiss or two!

I sometimes prefer chatting up English girls than Irish girls because if you chat up an Irish girl they always know somebody who knows somebody else and it's something you worry about. But I do love Irish girls. They're so friendly. You could meet a complete stranger and be like lifelong friends. Irish people are like that.

I like women like Jennifer Lopez. My ideal situation would be to be married to Jennifer Lopez and to go offside with Jennifer Love Hewitt!

The first thing I look for in a woman is her eyes. Piercing eyes amaze me. When the band started out I actually dated a fan. It went on for a while but it's too personal to reveal why we split up. It was a mutual decision.

So when people ask me if I would ever date a fan, I reply, 'Of course I would, haven't I done so already?'

I definitely, without a doubt, want to settle down and have kids. I'll hopefully settle down in the next three or four years.

At this stage, if this band split up tomorrow I'd have lived my life in such a short space of time, because I've seen most countries in the world, I've seen everywhere I wanted to. I've done almost everything I wanted to do. The only thing I've still to do is find a person that I'll spend the rest of my life with, settle down, buy a house, buy a car, go on holidays.

I don't think any other kids, except maybe Boyzone, have gone through what I have. But not even Boyzone really, because they started from the bottom and worked so hard

Mum's the Word

Patricia Egan on Kian

When Kian was younger he was a live wire. You always had to be careful where he was and what he was doing. He was much the same he is today – very lively – and you'd want to know where he was at all the time. The fact that I wasn't working outside the home meant I could keep a closer eye on him. He was very outgoing and still is; very friendly and makes friends easily. I was speaking to another mother recently and we were going back to when her lad was four or five and she remembered that where her son was shy, Kian wasn't. He'd be up to give her a kiss whenever he met her. He was never really a bold child, though – he did what he was told more or less.

Over the last year he's been the same Kian. He may have became a little wiser and perhaps more apprehensive in dealing with people. He isn't as quick now to answer questions as he was back when he was in school. I always felt that if anyone was going to get into trouble it would be Kian, but he didn't get into any major hassle in the end. I think all his energy went into the extra-curricular activities in the end. I suppose I was lucky that he concentrated on that aspect in life. He is great to me. He rings me up every day, sometimes twice, three times a day, to tell me any news.

I had Kian on stage from the age of four, and from that day – and this might sound very smug – I knew he'd end up on the stage somewhere. I do miss him a lot now, because he has that kind of personality. You always knew he was in the house; his friends would be around calling for him. Sometimes when I see him on the television I can't really believe it's him.

Mae Filan on Shane

As a little boy, Shane was always very lively and into music and he took leading parts in plays. Even though he was the youngest of seven, he was very capable from when he was little. He was a very loving child – no matter what you'd want Shane to do he'd just fly off and do it for you.

I would often expect Shane to be doing his homework and I'd find him upstairs singing; he was really into that. As a teenager he was very much into sport: rugby, Gaelic football, soccer and show-jumping. If you were in bad form or anything Shane would start telling a joke to cheer you up.

I always knew he would go into what he's doing now, though maybe not with such a big profile. I didn't expect him to be lucky enough to meet people like Louis Walsh and Ronan Keating. It was me, originally, that rang Louis. I'm from Kiltimagh and I knew Louis as a child. I knew that Shane had a talent but when I rang Louis I was just hoping that he might just get him into a band or something. I didn't know what to expect, otherwise I might have advised him to go back to college!

Despite the events of the past year Shane is still the same. I haven't noticed a difference, although he misses home and all that. It's a big world he's out in and he realises that he has to be careful and I'm sure he has learned a lot, now that he has travelled so much. When he went away at first I was more worried – I just didn't know what to expect or what they were really getting themselves into. But I don't worry about a thing because Anto, their tour manager, looks after them. He's like a father to those boys. And I know Louis and Ronan won't let anything go wrong, as long as the boys keep their heads on their shoulders and their feet on the ground.

Yvonne Byrne on Nicky

Nicky was a good-humoured and very affectionate boy. He was outgoing and confident from a very early age. I worried about Nicky when he was a teenager and I always knew where he was. If he was going to be out late, even now, when he is back in Ireland, he will ring and say, 'I won't be home until that time' or 'I got delayed' or 'I'm going to such a place'. He would always do that and likewise if he was babysitting for his brother Adam who is 12 years younger, and I said I'd be home at twelve or half twelve, he'd be worried if I didn't ring. I can never remember him getting into any sort of trouble in school, thank God. He wouldn't have been mischievous now in any way, maybe a bit of fun, but he was never in a lot of trouble.

When he was 16 he went away to Leeds and I suppose it took a lot out of us at that stage. We didn't want him to go until the following year, because he had just finished fifth year. He had only one year left in school, but we let him go because Leeds were very anxious to get him – they put us under a lot of pressure. I was always worried while he was there: I probably had the most expensive phone bill in Ireland – it's a bit cheaper now! I never really felt he'd fall in with the wrong crowd. When they were at Leeds they were very well looked after.

Over the past year, he's still been the same Nicky. He has a good head on his shoulders and always has had. He's also got Georgina to keep an eye out for him. When he was living at home he would always come in and say if anything happened, because I only had two of them for years, so we were – and still are – a close family and everything was discussed. Nicky's like that. He'd come in and tell you a joke if he was down in the pub or out with the lads, or whatever. He's living life now in the fast lane, but he still goes out of his way to call me no matter where he is.

Marie Feehily on Mark

Mark was the oldest of three boys but I didn't place any extra responsibility on him. He was always into tennis and won matches with the local club several times, and he played squash and badminton as well. He was very lively as a child. He always had to be on the go. He's never had any bother mixing or anything like that over the years. He was very much into music, from when he was three years of age.

Actually, on the last day of playschool, he amazed everybody. Instead of standing up and saying the normal nursery rhyme he stood up on the stage and sang 'Uptown Girl'. He was always interested in singing and took part in many shows over the years. He always had one of the main parts and he got great encouragement from the teachers in Summerhill College.

Mark never really had any problems when he was younger. He was always happy-go-lucky, easy-going, not really excitable at all. I don't worry too much about him now; they're in really safe hands and they're so well looked after. I would worry about him if he went into that business on his own, but the five of them are together as a team. I do miss him, though. It is a big break for Mark because he's a real home-bird altogether and always was. Even growing up he was never one to stay away at night; he would go out with his friends but he always came home.

The year he was doing the Leaving Cert, it really started to happen that year. It was just happening gradually from March on. I wouldn't let him turn down the chance – there was no way. He contacts me if not every day, then every second day. He wants to find out all the local news.

Mairead McFadden on Bryan

As a child Bryan was wild! He was a great kid growing up – a bit of a trickster. He put a stone into his ear one day when he was younger and my sister was minding him, and he had to go into Temple Street hospital to get it out. He was just wild! One second you'd look at him and the next he was at the top of a tree.

Susan and him got on brilliantly. He always looked out for her, but she's quiet. They were opposites when they were growing up. You'd always know he was in the house whereas she'd be in her room one day to the next and you wouldn't even know she was there.

I was actually very strict and I still am very strict with my children and Bryan was rarely allowed to go off our road; he could go round to the next road, where his best friend Edward lived, and that was it. My strictness paid off, because there are a lot of kids who come into our area from other areas and they're taken off at weekends by the police, who find them sitting down drinking cans in the streets.

Bryan did have a weight problem when he was younger. I don't think it ever actually came between him and his night's sleep, but it wasn't just that he had a weight problem – he actually never grew. He was always very small and then all of a sudden he sprouted up to over six foot and the weight just fell off him. He's about six foot two now.

He was very messy and untidy as a boy; he still is. He was home recently and I was away and I looked in his room when I got back and it was a complete mess. But he was a great kid, a very loveable kid. You could give out to him, you could even give him a clout and five minutes later he'd be back to you.

Bryan always wanted to sing. I said to him, 'Do your Leaving Cert, when you've got your Leaving Cert you can do what you want' – that is whatever job you want to do you can try it out. I'm delighted for him. He's very, very good and he would give you the shirt off his back – he is a very generous young fellow. It's actually a fault he has; there have been times when he might have a fiver in his pocket and if his friend hadn't got any money he'd give him half of it.

Kian Egan

DATE OF BIRTH: 29.4.1980
PLACE OF BIRTH: Sligo
STAR SIGN: Taurus
HEIGHT: 5ft 8ins
WEIGHT: 11st
COLOUR OF EYES: blue
WAIST SIZE: 32
SHOE SIZE: 8

Shane Filan

DATE OF BIRTH: 5.7.1979
PLACE OF BIRTH: Sligo
STAR SIGN: Cancer
HEIGHT: 5ft 9ins
WEIGHT: 11½st
COLOUR OF EYES: hazel green
WAIST SIZE: 31
SHOE SIZE: 9

Mark Feehily

DATE OF BIRTH: 28.5.1980
PLACE OF BIRTH: Sligo
STAR SIGN: Gemini
HEIGHT: 5ft 10ins
WEIGHT: 12st
COLOUR OF EYES: blue
WAIST SIZE: 34
SHOE SIZE: 9½

Nicky Byrne

DATE OF BIRTH: 9.10.1978
PLACE OF BIRTH: Dublin
STAR SIGN: Libra
HEIGHT: 5ft 9½ins
WEIGHT: 10½st
COLOUR OF EYES: blue
WAIST SIZE: 32
SHOE SIZE: 7½

Bryan McFadden

DATE OF BIRTH: 12.4.1980
PLACE OF BIRTH: Dublin
STAR SIGN: Aries
HEIGHT: 6ft 2ins
WEIGHT: 'Never mind!'
COLOUR OF EYES: blue
WAIST SIZE: 34
SHOE SIZE: 10

Tell Me . . .

IF YOU COULD BE ANYONE ELSE, WHO WOULD YOU BE?

Nicky: I'm quite happy with myself to be honest. I'm very lucky to be who I am and with what I have. But I wouldn't mind looking like Brad Pitt.
Mark: Winnie the Pooh! Just kidding! I don't know, I've never thought about it. I'm grateful for what I have.
Bryan: My dad.
Kian: Michael Jackson – for a day.
Shane: Someone starring opposite Catherine Zeta Jones.

WOULD YOU POSE NAKED FOR A MILLION POUNDS?

Nicky: I don't think so. But if it wasn't for a magazine that was in Ireland or England or Europe, I just might think about it.
Mark: Yeah, course I would!
Bryan: Yes.
Kian: Probably!
Shane: No, definitely not!

DESCRIBE YOUR HAPPIEST MOMENTS.

Nicky: I like big parties that involve my family and friends. Big get-togethers are always cool. Christmas in my house is the best time in the world.
Mark: When I'm at home having a great time with my family and friends and also getting the number one singles.
Bryan: Getting into the band was one of the greatest days of my life.
Kian: Being on stage, getting our number ones.
Shane: When I got into the band, meeting Louis and Ronan. Getting to number one.

ARE YOU SUPERSTITIOUS?

Nicky: Yes, very. Magpies, ladders, everything.
Mark: Yes, I am, very much so. Sometimes I've avoided walking under a ladder, stuff like that!
Bryan: Sometimes.
Kian: To a certain extent. I won't go under ladders but I don't believe in black cats.
Shane: I don't like walking under ladders and I count magpies if I see them.

WHAT DO YOU WEAR IN BED?

Nicky: Sometimes boxer shorts and sometimes nothing but a smile.
Mark: Boxer shorts.
Bryan: A smile.
Kian: Boxers.
Shane: Boxers.

WHAT WOULD YOU MOST LIKE TO WAKE UP IN BED WITH?

Nicky: My girlfriend, Georgina, of course.
Mark: Mariah Carey.
Bryan: Jennifer Love Hewitt.
Kian: Heather Graham.
Shane: Nicole Kidman or Catherine Zeta Jones.

WHEN DID YOU LAST CRY YOURSELF TO SLEEP AND WHY?

Nicky: When my cousin Kenneth died last year in a car crash.
Mark: When my grandad died. It was awful. I just couldn't believe it because one minute he was there and the next he was gone.

Bryan: When 'Swear It Again' went to number one. I had a few drinks in me!
Kian: Probably when I was about 16 and had broken up with my girlfriend.
Shane: I can't remember crying myself to sleep but the last time I cried was when I was leaving home earlier in the year, because my mother was crying.

WHAT'S THE FIRST THING YOU NOTICE ABOUT A PERSON?

Nicky: The first thing I notice about a girl is her eyes. I think girls' eyes are amazing. The first thing I notice about a guy is the way he is acting, i.e. does he like boy bands etc?
Mark: What they look like and if they're friendly.
Bryan: Their eyes.
Kian: Eyes and their smile.
Shane: Always the face.

WHAT IS YOUR FAVOURITE PART OF YOUR BODY?

Nicky: My left baby toenail. When it's freshly cut. Only joking – what sort of question is that?
Mark: My left eyebrow! Ah, no, I don't know.
Bryan: My eyes.
Kian: My eyes.
Shane: My hands.

WHAT IS YOUR FAVOURITE FILM?

Nicky: *Titanic* was good. *Die Hard* I love. Too many to mention.
Mark: *The Nutty Professor* and funny films like that.
Bryan: *Titanic*, *Patch Adams*.
Kian: *Titanic*.
Shane: *Titanic* or *Armageddon*.

WHAT IS YOUR FAVOURITE TV SHOW?

Nicky: *Friends*, or *The Den* and the *Late Late Show*. I can't believe Gay Byrne has left.
Mark: *Friends*, *Jerry Springer*, *South Park* and *The Simpsons*.
Bryan: *Friends*.
Kian: *Friends*.
Shane: *Friends*.

WHO IS YOUR FAVOURITE ACTRESS?

Nicky: Liz Hurley.
Mark: I think Lisa Kudrow [Phoebe in *Friends*] is very funny.
Bryan: Jennifer Love Hewitt.
Kian: Cameron Diaz.
Shane: Catherine Zeta Jones.

WHO IS YOUR FAVOURITE SINGER?

Nicky: Phil Collins or Madonna.
Mark: Mariah Carey and Michael Jackson.
Bryan: Stevie Wonder, Shania Twain.
Kian: AJ Backstreet.
Shane: George Michael or Michael Jackson.

NAME YOUR FAVOURITE BAND.

Nicky: Boyzone, Backstreet Boys, The Beach Boys are very cool.
Mark: Maybe Boyzone, Backstreet Boys, Destiny's Child, TLC or DRU Hill. I've loads and loads.
Bryan: Backstreet Boys.
Kian: Backstreet Boys.
Shane: Backstreet Boys, The Corrs.

HOW WOULD YOU DESCRIBE YOURSELF IN A PERSONAL COLUMN?

Nicky: Are you looking for somebody tall, dark, handsome with a good body? Well, skip me and look again 'cos that's not me!
Mark: Young Irish fellow is looking for a girl who can have a great laugh!
Bryan: Irish and desperate!
Kian: Small, cute, blue eyes, looking for love.
Shane: Young male, 5ft 9ins, dark hair and ready for action!

WHAT TURNS YOU ON?

Nicky: A girl dressed up in a police uniform. That just does it for me.
Mark: Sexy outfits and cheeky statements.
Bryan: My switch!
Kian: Lots of saucy things.
Shane: High-heeled shoes and short skirts.

HOW FAR WOULD YOU GO ON YOUR FIRST DATE?

Nicky: I wouldn't do a thing. Kiss and that's it.
Mark: It depends on the person and the situation.
Bryan: To the pub and back.
Kian: Not too far.
Shane: Just a kiss.

WHAT IRRITATES YOU MOST?

Nicky: Ignorant and arrogant people. People who think they are better than everyone else.
Mark: When the fans don't respect you and when people order you around.
Bryan: Arrogance.
Kian: Ignorant people.
Shane: I can't stand girls with smelly breath and girls with see-through high-heeled shoes where you can see their tights.

WHAT'S YOUR MOST PRIZED POSSESSION?

Nicky: My family and Georgina and, of course, my Siemens C25 mobile phone.
Mark: My family and my friends and my mobile phone.
Bryan: My family.

Kian: My mobile phone.
Shane: My car, a BMW.

HOW DO YOU KNOW YOU'RE IN LOVE?

Nicky: When your trousers become too tight! No, I'm only joking! I think when you feel you can't live without that person; she means so much to you.
Mark: When you'd do anything for the other person, no matter what, and as long as you love that person it doesn't matter what happens.
Bryan: When you think about nothing but the person you're in love with.
Kian: You just know it. You feel it inside.
Shane: I suppose when you can't live without the girl.

HAVE YOU FALLEN IN LOVE RECENTLY?

Nicky: Yeah, about five years ago.
Mark: Nope!
Bryan: Yes.
Kian: Not too recently.
Shane: I don't think I've ever been seriously in love.

WOULD YOU EVER WANT TO BE A MALE MODEL?

Nicky: I did some modelling before I joined Westlife. But it's not all it's made out to be.
Mark: No, I hate photo-shoots.
Bryan: No, I'm not good-looking enough.
Kian: I did it a couple of times, a few years ago.
Shane: I'd love to, but I don't know if I'd be tall enough.

IS ANY PART OF YOUR BODY PIERCED?

Nicky: No. I did have my ear pierced, but that was years ago.
Mark: Nope!
Bryan: No.
Kian: Yeah, my left ear.
Shane: No, and I hate piercing.

DO YOU HAVE ANY TATTOOS?

Nicky: Yes, on my lower back.
Mark: Nope!
Bryan: Yes.
Kian: Chinese writing on my left ankle which I got done in Sydney. It means 'spirit and soul'. It's tiny.
Shane: No, I won't get one of them.

IF YOU WERE TOLD YOU HAD A WEEK TO LIVE, WHAT WOULD YOU DO?

Nicky: I'd rob a car and be in a police chase. But, no, wait. I'd get someone else to rob a car 'cos I'd want to be driving the Garda car!

Mark: I'd go home and spend it with everyone.
Bryan: Spend it with my family.
Kian: I'd go on every scary rollercoaster in the world.
Shane: I'd spend it with my family and friends. I'd rob a bank – only joking.

WHAT TYPE OF UNDERWEAR DO YOU LIKE?

Nicky: Calvin Klein medium size, if anyone wants to purchase some for me!
Mark: Snug boxers.
Bryan: Clean underwear.
Kian: Calvin Klein.
Shane: Calvin Klein.

HAVE YOU EVER PLAYED SPIN THE BOTTLE?

Nicky: Yeah, years ago at Bayside train station and at the tennis courts. There used to be loads of us and loads of girls. We had a deadly time – those were the days.
Mark: Yes, once or twice.
Bryan: Oh, yes! One of my favourite pastimes!
Kian: I have.
Shane: Loads of times.

HAVE YOU EVER WATCHED A BLUE MOVIE?

Nicky: No, yeah, no, eh, I watched a green one!
Mark: I'm not telling you!
Bryan: Yes!
Kian: I have.
Shane: No!

ARE YOU A GOOD KISSER?

Nicky: If anyone wants to come to our hotel now and snog the five of us and give us marks out of ten, then tell them to call Louis or Ronan to arrange it.
Mark: I don't know. I suppose I try my best – you'll have to ask someone I kissed.
Bryan: Everyone has their own style.
Kian: I hope so.
Shane: I hope I'm not too bad.

IF A WAR BROKE OUT, WOULD YOU FIGHT FOR YOUR COUNTRY?

Nicky: Yes, I'd be a fighter pilot.
Mark: Yes, of course I would – but I don't like wars.
Bryan: No!
Kian: Maybe.
Shane: Definitely.

ARE YOU STILL A VIRGIN? IF SO, WHY?

Nicky: No, I am not. But don't let my mam read this!

Mark: You don't think I'm answering that, do you? I don't think so!
Bryan: No.
Kian: No.
Shane: Not telling you.

DO YOU WORK OUT IN A GYM?

Nicky: Yeah, I try to. But I hate running. I've run too much in my life already. We used to call Leeds, Leeds United Running Club.
Mark: Every now and then.
Bryan: No, well, sometimes.
Kian: I do.
Shane: The odd time, when I get a chance.

ARE YOU SELF-CONSCIOUS ABOUT YOUR APPEARANCE?

Nicky: Yes, I am now, since I've been in the band, and that's because you see so many bad photos of yourself that you try to change some things.
Mark: A little bit, but not very. I think everyone is a little bit.
Bryan: Yes!
Kian: I am.
Shane: A wee bit, but I have to be because we're in the public eye.

IF YOU WEREN'T IN WESTLIFE, WHAT WOULD YOU BE DOING NOW?

Nicky: I'd be driving a Garda car at high speed around Dublin, keeping the peace.
Mark: Probably in school, college. I'd still have a happy life.
Bryan: I'd be in a different band!
Kian: Probably teaching music.
Shane: Doing accountancy at college in Limerick.

WOULD YOU BE EMBARRASSED ABOUT GOING ON A NUDIST BEACH?

Nicky: Yeah, probably. But I'd do it for a laugh if all the lads came with me.
Mark: It depends who with!

Bryan: Yes!
Kian: No, but I wouldn't do it!
Shane: I wouldn't be able to do that, no way!

HAS ANYONE CLOSE TO YOU EVER DIED?

Nicky: Yes, my cousin Kenneth. He was only 21 and we were quite close. It annoys me to think his short life was snatched away from him.
Mark: Yes, a few people.
Bryan: Yes, my auntie and my teacher.
Kian: Grandparents.
Shane: Aunties and uncles, not immediate family.

WHICH STARS HAVE BEEN NICEST TO YOU?

Nicky: All the Boyzone lads, especially Ronan, Keith and Shane. They are really cool. Lee from 911 is really nice too, and Mel C from the Spice Girls.
Mark: Boyzone, Emma Bunton, Mel C, Bryan Adams, Geri Halliwell. Loads of them are nice.
Bryan: Bryan Adams, who is so down to earth and kind. He is a superstar. I'm a nobody and he still had time for me.
Kian: All of them, we're good friends with loads of bands.
Shane: Obviously Ronan. Backstreet Boys. Jamiroquai was really nice. Andrea Corr.

WHICH IS YOUR FAVOURITE METHOD OF RELAXATION?

Nicky: Lying down on the couch in my front room at home, watching a video with my family and Georgina, having a cup of tea.
Mark: Chilling out in my house or with my friends – just chatting and listening to music.
Bryan: A few beers.
Kian: Sitting down at home with friends and family.
Shane: Just lying back, chilling out, watching telly.

ARE YOU LEFT OR RIGHT HANDED?

All: Right.

WHAT IS YOUR BIGGEST FEAR?

Nicky: When I'm away, I worry that something

might happen to my family. I worry too much.
Mark: That something bad would happen to the people I'm close to.
Bryan: If something happened to my family.
Kian: That the band would split tomorrow.
Shane: That anything would happen to my family.

WHO IS YOUR FAVOURITE TV STAR?

Nicky: Dustin the turkey.
Mark: Eddie Murphy, Lisa Kudrow, Jennifer Aniston. I have many.
Bryan: Chandler from *Friends*.
Kian: Matt Le Blanc, who plays Joey in *Friends*.
Shane: Phoebe out of *Friends* [Lisa Kudrow].

ARE YOU AN EARLY RISER OR A NIGHT OWL?

Nicky: I'm a bit of both. I go to bed really late but I always get up on time.
Mark: A night owl.
Bryan: Both!
Kian: A night owl.
Shane: I'm a very late riser, but we're forced to get up early.

WHAT IS YOUR FAVOURITE COLOUR?

Nicky: Blue, white or black.
Mark: Green or black.
Bryan: Red or black.
Kian: Blue or white.
Shane: Black.

IF YOU COULD CHANGE ONE PART OF YOUR BODY, WHAT WOULD IT BE?

Nicky: I wouldn't change anything. I think you should be happy with what you have.
Mark: I'd get a smaller nose!
Bryan: Everything, except my heart and soul and mind.
Kian: My ears.
Shane: I haven't a clue.

WESTLIFE
ON . . .

Kian: It was brilliant. We were the first Irish act to have a number one in Britain at Christmas. We did the track 'I Have A Dream' for an Abba tribute TV show a while ago. I like their music. We recorded the Terry Jacks song 'Seasons In The Sun' because our manager Louis Walsh has always liked it.

Along with winning the Record of the Year award we were able to end the year feeling extremely happy. To achieve this was absolutely mad. I celebrated by going on a Caribbean holiday with my friends at Christmas. I asked my parents to book it. It was my first holiday in the sun and it was fantastic.

We only had 12 days off during the whole previous year. We all worked very hard and hope the year 2000 is just as rewarding.

Nicky: I was over the moon because I can remember watching the Spice Girls at number one with 'Two Become One' when I was still playing for Leeds. It still hasn't settled in. It doesn't seem like it's happening to us. I know it is, but I don't know, if you know what I mean! I spent the Christmas in Dublin and in Co. Donegal.

Bryan: It was amazing! I can remember watching the Spice Girls getting it before and just thought, 'What would it be like to get a Christmas number one?' We never even thought we'd be going for a Christmas number one or even release a single near Christmas. So when we won, it was the best feeling of all because we didn't think we were going to achieve that. We knew we'd have a chance of getting in the top three but we never expected this!

When I heard the news I was spending Christmas in Dublin, so I just had a few drinks to celebrate. The band wasn't together as we were all on holiday. So we rang to congratulate each other and we also contacted the producers to thank them for their help.

Shane: I was in Sligo spending the Christmas holidays with my family when I heard the news. I had a few drinks to celebrate. Everybody was really happy for us.

I think all our families, more than anyone else, were proud of us. I was just so proud as it was the last number one of the Millennium, as well and the first of the new one as well.

Mark: Winning the Record of the Year award and then a couple of weeks later getting the Christmas number one – who could ask for more at Christmas? Who could have asked for a better couple of weeks?

It was the group's first holiday for ages and after spending Christmas with my family in Sligo, I went to France.

Shane: It was definitely the best night for the band so far. We were delighted to be in the running, never mind winning it. After the first couple of votes it looked like ourselves and Ronan were kind of edging through and we were saying, 'Hold on, we're up against our manager here!'

It didn't matter who was second to us, even if it was Ronan. We wanted this award so much. With every vote we were jumping up and down. It was a real see-saw affair: Ronan would go ahead and then we'd go ahead and vice versa. Then we won – it was just unbelievable. We went upstairs and had a couple of drinks. We didn't go mad because we had to be up at 7a.m. the next morning.

Bryan: Getting the Christmas number one was brilliant, but I think getting the Record of the Year award was the best feeling so far. The Christmas number one is the best of the number ones, but the Record of the Year just topped it all. It wasn't about just selling singles – it was about the public voting what was the best song.

We didn't really talk to anyone before or during the award ceremony because everyone was so focused on their performance. We had a laugh with S Club 7

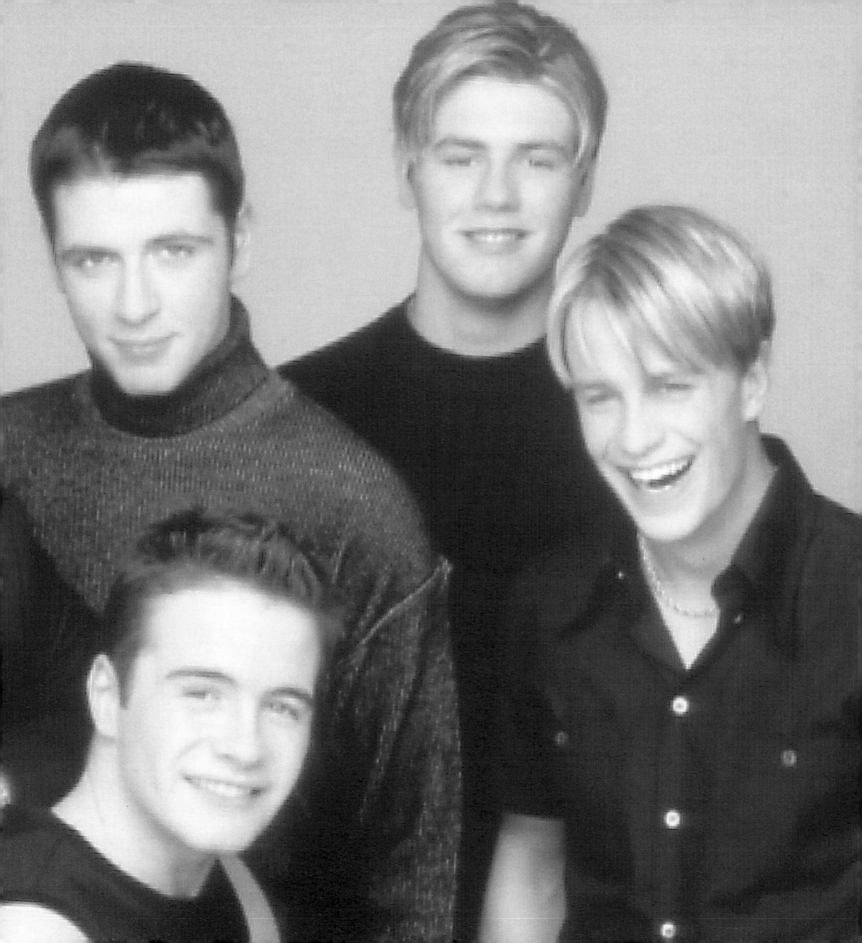

79

were in with a shout, but I never thought it would be ourselves. I'm still on a high.

Kian: We had no idea at all that we'd win. We went in being told that we were in the top ten records of the year. We thought if we got number six or seven we'd be very happy. The only place we didn't think we'd come was first!

I'm sure Ronan would have preferred to have won but Boyzone got the Record of the Year award last time around. It will be interesting to see who gets it next year.

We gave Ronan a big hug at the end and then went for a few drinks.

who were sitting at our table. We always have a great laugh with them and, of course, Ronan too.

I was in tears. I was so emotional. It was the best feeling of my life, like I'd really achieved something major.

Mark: To be honest, I didn't think we'd have any sort of chance of winning it. The main people I thought would win were Britney Spears, Ricky Martin or Lou Bega.

Not many people stayed on for the party as a lot of the performers, like ourselves, had to be up early the next morning. Although we hung around and had a good chat with Jennifer Lopez.

Nicky: It was definitely one of the best moments of our career. It kind of crossed us over to a bigger market. I thought Ronan, Britney Spears and Ricky Martin

MEETING QUEEN ELIZABETH AT THE ROYAL VARIETY SHOW LAST AUTUMN.

Shane: We were all lined up after the show with the other acts, waiting for the Queen. She came along to Mark and Nicky and said, 'Thanks for taking the time out to do the show.' Then Bryan says, 'Your dress is beautiful' and she said, 'Why, thank you.' Then she came along to me and Kian and said, 'What a beautiful song; a great cover version. I'm a very big fan of Abba.' And then she just walked off.

Mark: It was really weird because we'd never met royalty before and the security and the formality of the whole thing freaked us out a little. Every step the Queen took was planned to perfection. It was very weird, but it was an amazing experience.

Nicky: It was scary. I was very nervous thinking she was a member of the Royal family. We were told we had to say 'Your Majesty' and stuff like that. It was so bizarre: five Irish lads meeting the Queen and we were like, 'What do we say to her?' We thought let's just be nice and be respectful. We were afraid we'd say something wrong but it was a great day for us doing the Royal Variety Show.

Bryan: I said to her, 'Your dress is lovely' because everyone was being really shy and quiet and I wanted to say something besides 'Hello your Majesty.' I just wanted to say something. I think she was pleased because she said, 'Why thank you!'

Kian: She said, 'Lovely to meet you' and we said, 'Thank you very much', *blah blah blah*. She said, 'Very nice song, well done' and then we all know what Bryan said next!

Mark: It's a fact that we're a lot more used to working so closely now and we can go away for a lot longer without feeling too homesick. Before we'd be away for two weeks and we'd be dying to get home. But we still miss home. I think a lot of people in Ireland and Britain think that just because we're famous here that we're famous in every part of the world. But we're not very well known in America at the moment and we want to get the name Westlife known on that side of the world, so it's a good thing that we can be away for a long time without feeling *too* homesick.

Sometimes you're confined on a plane for 24 hours with the other lads and sometimes you're crammed into a car or a hotel room or whatever. We're just normal people. Sometimes we do bicker and argue but we never get physical with each other and that's definitely a good thing.

We're just like any other five friends and, of course, one or two of us have an argument here and there. But that's only normal given the pressure we're under.

Shane: I think America is a big priority for us this year. We've released 'Swear It Again' as our first single over there. We did three weeks promotion in America in January. It was really hard work but we seem to have become very popular there. We're just chuffed to be out there playing to an audience. After all, they're the ones that really count.

We're going to bring out four more singles this year in Ireland, the UK and all over Europe, the first of which is 'Fool Again'. The new album is due out in October. Then starting in February 2001 we're doing a six-month tour.

We want to beat every band that's out there. We want to be the biggest band of all time.

Nicky: I think we've matured so much. We're all only about 20-years-old and already we're dealing with accountants and bank managers. Its a lot of responsibility to take on.

Kian: I just hope our success can continue. Last year was just phenomenal. I don't think we could wish for a better year. If we can equal that or get anywhere near to the achievements of last year it would be great. But if we could *beat* that success — it would be absolutely amazing.

Bryan: We want to break into America, that's our big hope. We've been there a few times this year. Along with building our base in Europe, America is the place where we want to build on last year's achievements.

Shane: Romance is bad at the moment! It's getting on my nerves a bit. It hasn't been good for me lately and I spent St. Valentine's day with my mum and dad. Hopefully I'll find somebody soon.

We meet a lot of famous people but, to be honest, I kind of stay away from the famous ones. I'd just rather meet an normal girl who wasn't in the limelight all the time. But it's very hard to find someone to trust. You've just got to keep trying. I think that Nicky is very lucky.

Mark: It's a bit of a sore point at the moment. We're going from teenagers into adults and around that stage of your life I think that girls begin to play a big part in it. We don't get much chance to really get to know girls, let alone continue a meaningful relationship.

A lot of people in our position end up going out with people in other bands. I think that is because they understand a lot more than someone who is not part of the pop industry.

Nicky: I was quoted in one paper saying I'd leave the band if it came in the way of my relationship with Georgina. To be honest, I don't know where that came from. Whatever I said my words were totally twisted by the press. People who know me know that it is simply not true.

It is very difficult being away from Georgina a lot of the time. But because of the special relationship we have, she wouldn't let me leave the band for her. I wouldn't have to leave the band for her. I love what I do and I love her. So you could say that I have the best of both worlds.

Bryan: I did go out with Lene from Aqua but that's finished. It was only a couple of dates over a couple of weeks. She is older than me. Then I went out with Kerry from Atomic Kitten. We're still good mates. We've known Atomic Kitten for a long time and we share the same hotels when we're on tour. We always have a drink and a laugh.

Around Christmas time I asked Kerry out on a date and we went out a couple of times in Dublin and Manchester. The two of us went into town and got snapped by photographers and all of a sudden we're 'boyfriend and girlfriend'. It can get a bit annoying when you can't even have friends. Although we've split up and remain good friends, in some people's minds we're still going out.

Kian: There's nobody at the minute. I was out on a date a few weeks before Christmas. I got on very well with her but it just didn't work out. Apart from that there is nothing definite. But I'm still looking!